WILL MY Child BE READY?

MISSIONARY PREP FOR MOMS

EDITED BY

EMILY FREEMAN AND **MERRILEE BOYACK**

CONTRIBUTING AUTHORS:
DEANNE FLYNN • **WENDY ULRICH**
ROSEMARY LIND • **LESLIE OSWALD**

DESERET
BOOK

Compilation and text created by authors © 2015 Emily Freeman and Merrilee Browne Boyack

Visit us at DeseretBook.com

Library of Congress Cataloging-in-Publication Data

(CIP on file)
ISBN 978-1-62972-043-2

Printed in the United States of America
PubLitho, Draper, Utah

10   9   8   7   6   5   4   3   2   1

For every mother who has knelt in prayer for her child.
We are all in this together.

CONTENTS

CONTENTS

INTRODUCTION

The knock came late one night in May. I turned on the porch light and opened the door to find a high school boy standing there—baseball cap pulled down over his hair, shaggy beard, tears rolling down his cheeks. "Is Coach here?" he asked, eyes questioning and voice soft and humble. I invited him in and went to get Greg out of bed.

They talked in the basement for an hour and a half, the boy pouring out his heart and the coach mostly just listening. Finally, at the end of the conversation, the boy asked the question that had brought him to our door in the first place: "I want to change my life. I want to start going to church. I want to do what Garett did—serve a mission. Can you help me?"

And so the journey began.

This boy who hadn't attended church regularly in over six years, who had never read the Book of Mormon, who had just started saying his prayers, began to turn his life around.

It was our privilege to watch the Lord take the heart of this humble boy and turn him into a missionary. In February, just nine months after that knock on our door, he turned in his mission papers. In July he left for the Indiana Indianapolis Mission.

I don't know where you are in the process of preparing a child for a mission. Perhaps you have young children and are hoping to begin the mission training process at the beginning, or maybe your situation is more like the one above—you have less than a year to pull all the pieces together. Here is the good news: the path of preparing a child for a mission begins wherever you are. The most important thing to remember is that the Lord will help you in whatever your situation is. He will hasten the process if necessary. He will know just how to help you prepare your child for this great work.

Perhaps you could consider this book a conversation between mothers—tidbits of learning shared from mother heart to mother heart. The chapters have been written by mothers—all who have sent children out on missions and some who have served with their husbands presiding over missions and had the opportunity to mother hundreds of missionaries. Our most important advice is simply this: don't worry about what you have or haven't accomplished up to this point. Start where you are. When we gathered together as mothers to put down these thoughts, our biggest concern was that we would overwhelm you. On the other hand, we didn't want to leave out something that might make a difference in the preparation process. So we included everything that we thought might prove helpful and we now place it in your hands, with this caveat: read with the Spirit to know which parts will be helpful to you in preparing your child. Use this book as a resource, not as a prescriptive guide. Come back and consult it over time. Each mom is different, and each child is different. You may find that one chapter works well for one child, and another chapter is just what you need for another child. Our hope is that this resource, combined with promptings from the Spirit and advice from priesthood leaders, will give you added strength as you prepare your son or daughter to serve the Lord.

You are about to immerse yourself in a book focused on training up a missionary for the Lord. But before we jump in, it is important to pause and consider one of the most important factors in that training—you. Your efforts will be combined with the efforts of bishops, youth leaders, seminary teachers, family, and friends. However, next to the Spirit, you and your spouse will play one of the most crucial roles.

Because of that, this introduction is dedicated to you.

Your influence is immeasurable. Your errand is divine. Your responsibility is significant.

"Remember, in the world before we came here, faithful women were given certain assignments. . . . While we do not now remember the particulars, this does not alter the glorious reality of what we once agreed to. You are accountable for those things which long ago were expected of you just as are those we sustain as prophets and apostles!" (Spencer W. Kimball, "The Role of Righteous Women," *Ensign,* Nov. 1979, 102).

Surely one of the assignments given to many women was to raise up young men and young women who would be prepared to further the work of the Lord. A favorite Book of Mormon account tells of a powerful group of faithful women whose dedicated training led to miraculous experiences for their sons. You know their sons well. We refer to them as the Army of Helaman—the Stripling Warriors.

But what do you know of their mothers?

"Yea, they had been taught by their mothers, that if they did not doubt, God would deliver them. And they rehearsed unto me the words of their mothers, saying: We do not doubt *our mothers knew it*" (Alma 56:47–48; emphasis added).

What was it that their mothers knew?

Have you ever studied the process of conversion that allowed those women to become the mothers they were?

Throughout the book of Alma we observe several defining characteristics about those mothers, who were part of a group known as the Anti-Nephi-Lehies. They were raising children in a world fraught with challenge. It was a time filled with dissensions, intrigue, and most dangerous circumstances (see Alma 53:9). These mothers were acutely aware of the dangers, afflictions, and tribulations that their families faced. In an effort to strengthen the Lord's cause, they prepared their sons to enter the front lines of battle. Their actions defined their testimony. These were women who

- Were firm in the faith of Christ.
- Had been converted unto the Lord by the power and word of God.

- Were given a portion of God's Spirit.
- Had soft hearts.
- Were perfectly honest and upright.
- Knew how to repent and forgive through the merits of Christ.
- Were distinguished for their zeal toward God.
- Knew that God loved them.
- Knew that God loved their children.
- Were visited by angels.
- Kept covenants.
- Were firm in their beliefs.
- Never did fall away.
  (*See Alma 24, 27, 53; see also 3 Nephi 6:14.*)

Consider that list for a minute. Does that list describe you? What would you need to change to become more like those mothers? What would you need to learn?

One thing is certain—in order to raise Stripling Warriors we must become Stripling Mothers. We must live by the spiritual habits, behaviors, and principles we want our children to live by. Every day. That way, when our children encounter moments of doubt, which they surely will, they will be able to look to us as mothers and remember what we know to be true.

The task of training up a missionary for the Lord can seem overwhelming. However, the Lord will enable us to accomplish this great undertaking. The scriptures are a trusted resource. Living in tune with the Spirit will help us fulfill our divine responsibility. Learning from the counsel of current prophets and apostles of the Lord will also provide essential guidance. And turning to each other for inspiration and support will help sustain us.

We must remember that every child is unique, with different strengths and weaknesses. Each path will follow a different course. Sometimes we will encounter detours and even unanticipated outcomes.

The Spirit understands the needs of each child. Promptings will come as to how to guide, strengthen, and prepare each child to become the Lord's instrument—however, wherever, and whenever they may serve.

There may be times when you wonder if any good will come from your efforts. Don't give up! Your work is of the utmost importance, and heaven's attention will be constant.

The Lord is hastening His work. This hastening affects more than just the rising generation. He needs more than young men and young women who are willing to serve. He needs righteous mothers who will train them.

He needs you.

You will notice that the Book of Mormon does not call out any of the Stripling Mothers by name. They were united as a group of women with a great desire to prepare their children for the momentous task ahead of them. The same is true today. May we gather together as mothers, willing to share our belief as we prepare our children to go forward in faith, knowing the Lord will be with them.

Children who will not doubt.

Children who have been strengthened by mothers who knew.

"We do not doubt *our mothers knew it*."

10 THINGS I WISH I HAD
LEARNED BEFORE MY MISSION

1. **I WISH I WOULD HAVE PRAYED LONGER, MORE FERVENTLY, AND MORE SPECIFICALLY FOR THINGS THAT I NEEDED.** I feel like my prayers have become strengthened in all of those areas during my mission. Although they are not perfect, I feel like I have more of a conversation with God and less of a prayer list. I love listening to investigators and new converts pray because they are truly talking to their Heavenly Father, and you can tell. It's powerful.

2. **I WISH I WOULD HAVE STUDIED AND LEARNED.** Before my mission I felt like I studied the scriptures, but looking back I wish I would have learned how to feast on the good word of God. He has always provided for me when I go to the scriptures with a need or desire or looking for something. I wish I would have taken that approach more. Although I studied before my mission, I wish I would have truly feasted.

3. **I WISH I WOULD HAVE BEEN MORE OF A MISSIONARY.** Looking back I can remember different people that I could have helped or influenced more with the testimony I had at the time. You never know who you could help develop a testimony unless you share yours. You have something to share. Never forget that.

4. **I WISH I WOULD HAVE MAGNIFIED MY CALLINGS.** This one is big. One thing that I always want to do and wish I would have done better is magnify the calling that I was given. If you are in a calling, be accountable for that calling and stand up for what you believe in— all the time.

5. **I WISH I WOULD HAVE LEARNED HOW TO GET ANSWERS TO PRAYERS.** I should have put more time into getting specific answers to prayers. Knowing that what I do in my life is what God wants me to do is a powerful thing. I know that He will always guide us if we but ask.

6. **I WISH I WOULD HAVE BEEN MORE FAITHFUL TO MY COVENANTS.**
   I realize now I could have studied better the covenants I made when I
   was baptized and when I received the priesthood. I wish I would have
   learned and studied deeper about the oath and covenant and what I
   promised when I was baptized. Both of those are so important, and if we
   truly understand them, we will never fail.

7. **I WISH I WOULD HAVE BETTER UNDERSTOOD WHAT IT MEANT TO TAKE
   THE NAME OF CHRIST UPON ME.** It is important to know what it means
   to be a representative of Jesus Christ and to do as He would do. True men
   and women are the ones that stand up for the virtues and standards of
   others and don't knock them down. They are the ones who act like Christ
   and don't just say they do. They are like the Savior and try to be more like
   Him each day.

8. **I WISH I WOULD HAVE LEARNED HOW TO TEACH.** I should have taken
   my responsibilities to teach classes and home teaching more seriously.
   I could have put more effort into those teaching assignments and really
   learned how to teach using questions, listening, and responding to needs.

9. **I WISH I WOULD HAVE WORKED HARDER.** Enough said. Learn how to
   go hard in everything you do and learn the importance of accountability.
   When you are accountable you are responsible for the outcome, so you
   don't make excuses or murmur. Do what you are supposed to do, work
   hard, and learn how to be accountable so that the Lord can trust you in
   His vineyard.

10. **I WISH THAT I WOULD HAVE STUDIED THE LIFE OF CHRIST MORE AND
    WHAT THE ATONEMENT IS.** It is truly through the Atonement that our
    lives can change. It is through the gospel that we become better. It is
    through the gospel that we become true men and women. As we exercise
    faith and work hard, the Lord will change us for the better. He will teach
    us what we need to know, but first we need to know Him and know
    what He can do for us. Everything in this life is dependent on our Savior,
    Jesus Christ. He is the reason we can be happy and truly enjoy this life,
    and He loves each one of us to the very core.

CHAPTER 1

I WILL DO THE THING
THE LORD COMMANDS
Emily Freeman

"And they were also distinguished for their zeal towards God, and also towards men; for they were perfectly honest and upright in all things."
ALMA 27:27

One afternoon I heard my sons arguing in the toy room. I leaned over the railing and yelled down the stairway for them to try to work it out. My suggestion went unheeded, so I leaned over the railing again. This time I yelled for Caleb to come to the bottom of the stairs. He was the oldest at four years old, and thus he qualified as the most responsible. "Caleb," I said, "You need to choose the right."

"I am, Mom," he said with the utmost sincerity. "But Josh is on the left."

Choosing the right is one of the most important principles we can teach our children early in their lives. William D. Oswald, second counselor in the Sunday School general presidency, taught that obedience is "the first law of Heaven" (*Ensign*, Jan. 2008, 10). Obedience may be the first law, but as mothers we must remember that obedience is learned. Consider Alma and the sons of Mosiah: these men became some of the most powerful missionaries of all time, and yet they weren't born with obedience; in fact, they struggled with it. They were boys who learned the meaning of obedience after walking a really rough road. Their life experiences helped them to understand the blessings and the consequences that came from every choice they made.

A simple way we can begin teaching our children obedience is by creating a list of rules for our home. Through this process our children will quickly begin to recognize that there are privileges for following the rules and consequences for breaking them. We must teach our children that the same is true of the commandments of God. There are blessings predicated upon God's laws. Our obedience allows us to experience those privileges. Our disobedience leads to the consequences that follow poor choices.

In our home we have a catchphrase that reminds us of this principle. When one of us is struggling with a rule or a principle, we ask one simple question: "Are you above the law?" The phrase came from an experience that happened after one of our sons received a speeding ticket. When he returned home that evening and told us about his ticket, we asked him what the speed limit was. He told us it was 55 miles an hour. "How fast were you going?" we asked. He replied with a number way above that amount. "What do you think the purpose for the speed limit sign is?" I asked him.

"I don't know," he replied. Then after thinking about it for a minute, he said, "For protection, I guess."

"Right," I said. "For your protection and the protection of everyone around you. The sign is for everyone—every single driver on that road. It's there to protect you and every single driver on that road. It's a law. So, what was it that made you think you didn't have to follow the rule that everyone else was following? Are you above the law?"

Since then our family has joked about that line. We repeat it often when someone is making a decision that isn't necessarily obedient. *Are you above the law?* It makes us stop and think. It helps us realign our focus. It also helps us to remember that there is a difference between near obedience and exact obedience—there's a difference in the level of diligence and a difference in the blessings that follow. Elder D. Todd Christofferson teaches, "As we walk in obedience to the principles and commandments of the gospel, we enjoy a continual flow of blessings promised by God. . . . In times of distress, let your covenants be paramount and let your obedience be exact. Then you can ask in faith, nothing wavering, according to your need, and God will answer" ("The Power of Covenants," *Ensign,* May 2009, 21–22). Exact obedience is more than just living the letter of the law or going through the motions or checking a box on a list. It is a deeper understanding of the spirit of the law and obeying the principle with complete devotion. It is not enough to teach our children just the principle of obedience; it is crucial that they learn to recognize and anticipate the blessings that are obtained from living obediently.

Missionary Letter

"THIS NEXT MONTH we really want to see a miracle and get 40 baptisms before the 1st of June. That's when we will be holding the 40th anniversary celebration of the church in the former Yugoslavia. Right now we have 12 baptisms. In order to qualify ourselves as a mission for that kind of miracle we decided to do everything in our power to be EXACTLY obedient, as a mission. Desire, obedience, belief, trust that God will deliver. That's faith. It will be an exciting month."

Learning to Be Obedient

The stripling warriors were a group of young men who knew the importance of obedience and obtained blessings because of their diligence to that principle. "They were all young men, and they were exceedingly valiant for courage, and also for strength and activity; but behold, this was not all—they were men who were true at all times in whatsoever thing they were entrusted. Yea, they were men of truth and soberness, for they had been taught to keep the commandments of God and to walk uprightly before him" (Alma 53:20–21). this is your work

Several phrases stand out as being synonymous with obedience in that verse—*exceedingly valiant, true at all times,* and *taught to keep the commandments of God.* This dedication to obedience proved to be a great blessing in the young men's lives. Their obedience led to an increase of faith, was a means of protection, and was a precursor to miracles.

At the end of the great battle, Helaman counted his 2,060 warriors, and to his great astonishment, not one soul of them had perished: "And now, their preservation was astonishing to our whole army. . . . And we do justly ascribe it to the miraculous power of God, because of their exceeding faith in that which they had been taught to believe—that there was a just God, and whosoever did not doubt, that they should be preserved by his marvelous power. Now this was the faith of these of whom I have spoken; they are young, and their minds are firm, and they do put their trust in God continually" (Alma 57:26–27).

Missionary Letter

"I HAVE BEEN THINKING a lot about the importance of having a firm mind. A man with a firm mind has faith. He doesn't doubt when the unexpected happens. A man with a firm mind is positive; he doesn't let fear or disappointment cloud his abilities. A man with a firm mind is focused, leading to the accomplishing of goals realized because of steadfast determination. A firm mind isn't clouded by temptation, but rather visualizes the blessings and promises of God and presses forward to achieve them. 100% focus 100% of the time. Like the power of light when focused through a magnifying glass. Controlled power."

These young boys had exceeding faith in that which they had been taught, and their minds were firm. They had lived lives of obedience, and through their obedience they qualified for the blessings of faith, protection, and miracles.

How do we develop that kind of obedience in our own children? Perhaps there are lessons we can learn from the stripling warriors. These young men had been taught to keep the commandments of God. It is important to notice four important words in that phrase: *they had been taught.* As we teach the commandments to our children we must focus on two aspects: the *how* and the *why*. It is important for our children to understand *how* to live the commandments, what it looks like, what actions are required. But it is even more important for them to understand *why*. Teaching the *why* requires us to help them discover the doctrine. "True doctrine, understood, changes attitudes and behavior" (Boyd K. Packer, "Little Children," *Ensign*, Nov. 1986, 17).

Teaching the *How* and *Why* of Obedience

Here is an example of the *how* and the *why*. Have you ever noticed that missionaries are easily recognizable? You can quickly pick them out of a crowd or recognize them as they walk down the street. There is more than just a two-inch name badge that defines them—their whole appearance testifies of their mission. Missionaries are clean cut, modest, and dressed in Sunday best. Elders wear a white shirt and tie. Their outward appearance speaks of their inward beliefs. This is the *how* of dressing like a missionary. But it is hard to talk a teenager into dressing that way unless they understand the *why*.

Elder Boyd K. Packer teaches: "Do you know what 'Sunday best' means? It used to be the case. Now we see ever more informal, even slouchy, clothing in our meetings, even in sacrament meeting, that leads to informal and slouchy conduct" ("The Unwritten Order of Things," BYU Devotional Address, Oct. 15, 1996). From the moment our children are born, we can help them understand the meaning of "Sunday best." We do this as we help them prepare for worship every Sunday. The clothing we wear as we prepare to serve the Lord is part of living obediently and should represent what we believe. A white shirt and tie and modest clothing set one apart as a disciple of the Lord. That is the *why*.

Clothing is certainly not the only characteristic that sets missionaries apart. Their outward actions also define their role. These are young men and women who know what it means to live the *For the Strength of Youth* guidelines. Their language and their actions also represent their beliefs. Consider what makes an obedient missionary—waking on time, following rules, living standards, studying scriptures, keeping appointments, and testifying of Christ. The same is true for our children no matter what age they are. Their obedience includes

- Learning proper sleep habits.
- Following family and Church rules.
- Living the standards outlined in the *For the Strength of Youth* booklet.
- Attending seminary.
- Attending school.
- Showing up for work.
- Going to church.
- Serving and testifying of Christ.

Our children need to learn these eight habits long before their mission application is turned in. Remember, you will not be there on the mission to wake up your child, talk him or her into attending church meetings, or convince him or her to show up for work. Children need to learn to do those things on their own before they go on their missions. Obedience to these principles will help mold them into diligent and obedient missionaries.

Our children are very familiar with what missionaries look like, but perhaps they are not as familiar with what missionaries act like. One of the best ways for our children to learn how missionaries act is to invite them into our home. As members, we can share referrals, provide meals, and offer rides. We can also invite recently returned missionaries into our homes to teach family home evening lessons about their experiences. As children associate with these missionaries, they will begin to learn what obedience and diligence *look* like. They will have examples to follow and servants of the Lord they can look up to and emulate.

Choosing to Be Valiant

The stripling warriors were exceedingly valiant for courage, strength, and activity. *Valiant* is a word that is defined as "marked by courage or determination." These young men were determined. They had firm minds. They walked uprightly. I envision a group of boys who had become valiant warriors long before they approached the front lines of battle. The same must be true of our youth today. They must become missionaries long before they enter the Missionary Training Center. Their determination to serve will lead to increased obedience, and that determination can begin at a very young age.

"The single most important thing you can do to prepare for a call to serve is to *become* a missionary long before you *go* on a mission. Please notice that . . . I emphasized *becoming* rather than *going.* . . . It is possible . . . to *go* on a mission and not *become* a missionary, and this is not what the Lord requires or what the Church needs. My earnest hope for each of you . . . is that you will not simply go on a mission—but that you will become missionaries long before you submit your mission papers, long before you receive a call to serve, long before you are set apart by your stake president, and long before you enter the MTC" (David A. Bednar, "Becoming a Missionary," *Ensign,* Nov. 2005, 45).

It is important to recognize that being exactly obedient does not mean living perfectly. The stripling warriors were known as boys who were true at all times in whatsoever thing they were entrusted. That's what they were known for, but that doesn't mean they didn't make mistakes. In my mind, it means they knew how to correct their mistakes and then continue forward on the path of obedience—the path that they became known for. They knew what to do after making a mistake and how to move forward again. atonement

In our basement we have a quotation taken from my daughter's basketball coach during a time-out at a very intense basketball game. Coach

Hays said, "I know you are going to make mistakes. It's what you do after the mistake that I care about. It's how you recover."

One of the most important lessons we can teach regarding the principle of obedience is the principle of repentance. Obedience and repentance are two principles that go hand in hand. Our children need to understand that everyone is going to make mistakes. What is important is knowing how to recover from those mistakes. Alma the Younger recovered. The sons of Mosiah recovered. Those boys went on to serve amazing missions and accomplish extraordinary things. Their mistakes were of lesser importance; their willingness to recover and then obey was of greatest importance. It led to an increase of faith. It led to miracles. —recovery—healing

Do your children know how to recover? Do they know what it means to repent? Do they understand the role of the Atonement, the power of grace, the mission of the Savior? As you teach obedience, make sure you spend time teaching about second chances, and third chances. Teach them that the Savior offers them every chance. The Lord wants us to recover because He wants us to succeed. It doesn't matter how many times it takes us to get it right, as long as we are trying. If we are always trying, then we are always true—even if we make a mistake. Our obedience comes from our determination to be exceedingly valiant. And from that obedience, great blessings will come.

WHAT THEY NEED TO KNOW:

- Obedience is the first law of heaven.
- Obedience must be learned.
- Obedience leads to an increase of faith.
- Obedience is a means of protection.
- Obedience is a precursor to blessings and miracles.
- Obedience and repentance are principles that go hand in hand.

WHAT THEY NEED TO DO:

- Discover the *how* and the *why* behind the commandments.

- Learn how to follow rules.
- Live within the law.
- Willingly attend seminary, school, work, and church without prompting.
- Dress and act in a way that reflects their understanding of obedience.
- Recognize the blessings that come from obedience.

♥ WHAT THEY NEED TO BE:

"And they were all young, . . . and they were exceedingly valiant for courage, and also for strength and activity; but behold, this was not all—they . . . were true at all times in whatsoever thing they were entrusted. . . . for they had been taught to keep the commandments of God and to walk uprightly before him" (Alma 53:20–21).

FROM THE MISSIONARY HANDBOOK

"As you obey with a willing heart (see D&C 64:34), you will show the Lord your love for Him, earn the trust and confidence of members and nonmembers, and qualify for the companionship of the Holy Ghost (see John 14:15–17, 21; 1 Nephi 10:17; D&C 121:45–46)" ("Your Calling," *Missionary Handbook,* 3).

CHAPTER 2

TEACH ME ALL THAT I MUST DO
Merrilee Boyack

*"And rather than spend their days in idleness
they would labor abundantly with their hands."*
ALMA 24:18

It's Saturday morning and the Mormon Tabernacle Choir is playing gently in the background. Our four sons wake up and happily skip to the kitchen. After a nutritious breakfast, they beg to do their weekly chores. Off they go, singing and whistling as they complete their tasks without complaint.

Oh wait, that was the dream portion of my Saturday morning. Let's actually talk reality.

It's Saturday morning, and because I grew up in Detroit, Motown music is playing loudly in the background. We call to the kids to get out of bed and they drag in one by one. After breakfast, they slowly trudge off to do their work. But work they do. Because in our home, everyone works.

I always worried when returned missionaries proclaimed happily in their talks that their mission was the best time of their life. I just didn't want my kids to get the wrong impression. So I was delighted when one missionary added, "And it was also the hardest two years. I have never worked harder in my entire life." Thank you, honest missionary!

One of my favorite souvenirs from my sons' missions is their shoes. Each pair is similar—marked with holes, cracks, and worn leather, reflecting the hours and hours of hard work they poured into their missions.

Missions are hard work. Let's face it—our children will be paired up with complete strangers, put on a rigorous schedule, and probably walk or bike more than they ever have in their life. They must be prepared for the sheer rigor of a mission. And you, as their mom, are the perfect one to prepare them.

First, we must teach our children that work is good. This is certainly not an innate understanding. It takes some convincing to teach a child that working has an upside.

Such lessons began in the dawn of our earth's existence. God, in explaining Adam and Eve's new reality, told them, "By the sweat of thy face shalt thou eat bread, until thou shalt return unto the ground" (Moses 4:25). And then they went to work: "And it came to pass that after I, the Lord God, had driven them out, that Adam began to till the earth, and to have dominion over all the beasts of the field, and to eat his bread by the sweat of his brow, as I the Lord had commanded him. And Eve, also, his wife, did labor with him" (Moses 5:1).

> ## Missionary Letter
>
> "LIFE IS GOOD here in Georgia, minus the fact that we have to walk a lot. Thank goodness my mom taught me that I could walk 15 miles in one day before I came on my mission!"

Teaching Our Children to Work Hard

Just as Heavenly Father insisted that His children work, so should we. In fact, our prophet has taught us quite clearly: "Mothers, share household duties. It is often easier to do everything yourself than to persuade your children to help, but it is so essential for them to learn the importance of doing their share" (Thomas S. Monson, "Constant Truths for Changing Times," *Ensign,* May 2005, 20).

President Hinckley gave similar advice: "Work together. I don't know how many generations or centuries ago, someone first said, 'An idle mind is the devil's workshop.' Children need to work with their parents—to wash dishes with them, to mop floors with them, to mow lawns, to prune trees and shrubbery, to paint and fix up and clean up and do a hundred other things where they will learn that labor is the price of cleanliness and progress and prosperity" (*Teachings of Gordon B. Hinckley* [1997], 707).

President Spencer W. Kimball gave my favorite counsel: "It is right to work. Every man and woman and child should work. Even little children should learn how to share, to help do the housework and yardwork, to plant gardens, to plant trees, to pick fruit, and to do everything that needs to be done because that makes strong characters out of them and builds their faith and character. We want you parents *to create work* for your children" (*Teachings of Spencer W. Kimball,* 360; emphasis added). We loved to tell our children that if we couldn't find work for them, we would create it!

In fact, we have been known to post these quotes right above the chore chart to let our children know that their parents follow the prophets!

One of our most important roles as mothers is to encourage our children to work and to work hard so that they will build up the stamina and strength that are needed for a successful mission. This learning can only be earned drop by drop through personal experience. As they work, be sure and teach them the blessings that come from giving something their whole effort and then reaping the rewards. Encourage them in their efforts and then congratulate them for their work. Over time, they will learn deep within themselves of the goodness of work.

Being Prepared to Be Independent

An essential part of preparing our children to serve a mission is teaching them how to take care of themselves. A truly prepared missionary needs to be taught the life skills that are involved in being an adult and living completely on your own. Part of this preparation involves snipping the apron strings. Bit by bit, we must let go and let our children take command of their lives. They must be able to function independently by the time they walk out the door to serve their mission. "Generally, a young person who has been allowed to take responsibility

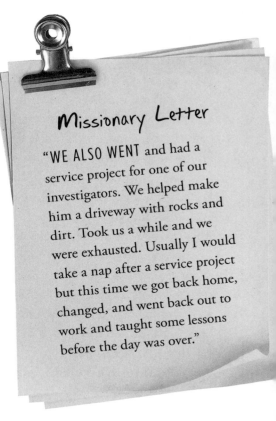

Missionary Letter

"WE ALSO WENT and had a service project for one of our investigators. We helped make him a driveway with rocks and dirt. Took us a while and we were exhausted. Usually I would take a nap after a service project but this time we got back home, changed, and went back out to work and taught some lessons before the day was over."

and develop appropriate independence will have an easier time adjusting to missionary service. This means that it is important for parents to nurture their children in such a way that encourages independent, responsible decision-making skills founded on gospel principles" (Robert K. Wagstaff, "Preparing Emotionally for Missionary Service," *Ensign,* Mar. 2011, 23–24).

Imagine a young man or woman who has not been taught these things being sent on a mission. All of a sudden, they find themselves in the MTC. They have no idea how to wash their clothes because Mom always did it. They go out into the mission field and have no idea how to cook because Mom always did it. They have never managed their own money and have no idea how to handle a bank account because Mom always did it. This poor missionary carries an added burden—not only is he or she trying to learn how to be a missionary in a foreign environment with a new companion, he or she also has no idea how to be self-sufficient and independent. So while other missionaries are learning the language, this missionary is learning how to iron a shirt or blouse.

Now let's imagine a young man or woman who has been fully trained and taught by a loving mother being sent on a mission. This missionary is comfortable doing the laundry, handling money, shopping, cooking, and a myriad of other things, because he or she has been doing these things for years. This missionary is *prepared* to hit the ground running on his or her mission. Plus, because they have been taught and trained in life skills, such missionaries have the confidence that goes along with that training. They are prepared to be leaders and prepared to help others.

To prepare your children well, it is important to teach and train them to be able to take care of themselves before they turn 18. As they grow, turn over to them the responsibility of their own care bit by bit. Specifics will vary for each child, but make a plan for your children. For example, you might decide that at age 7 they should be able to pack their lunch. Let them. At age 10 they could start learning to do their own laundry. Let them. At about age 14 they could get their own bank account and debit card. Let them.

Elder M. Russell Ballard, when serving as a mission president, asked his missionaries to respond to the question "What could my mother have done to better prepare me?"

"They said: 'Somehow Mom should have insisted that I pay more attention when she was trying to teach me about housekeeping—cooking, cleaning, laundry, bargain shopping, personal hygiene, mending, quick recipes, to name just a few.' To be an effective missionary one must be spiritually in tune, but the temporal well-being of the missionary becomes far more important than perhaps most of us realize. . . .

"May I suggest to you wonderful mothers that you put your arms around your children, look them squarely in the eye, and tell them to learn these skills because you want them to be happy and successful on their mission. What son or daughter will not respond to the loving eyes of his or her mother?" ("The Making of a Missionary," *Ensign,* Nov. 1976, 88).

For missionaries, stepping foot into the Missionary Training Center can be a challenging or even traumatic event. They have entered a completely new lifestyle and a foreign environment. Missionaries are usually sent to a place that is unfamiliar to them, often having to eat food that is new and different, many speaking a language that is completely new and facing cultures that are totally different from anything they have ever known.

Added to that is the change in lifestyle. No longer can they text a friend, scroll through Facebook to see what everyone is doing, listen to music on their cell phone to unwind, or post a funny picture on Instagram. They must conform to new rules—they can't jump in a car and take a ride or go for a hike. They will learn to spend time with a person they have never met who is now assigned to be their constant companion. Such a tremendous change in lifestyle and environment can be a huge shock and can lead to significant challenges.

Our children need to learn how to de-stress in ways they can use on their mission—reading scriptures, praying, singing, walking, and other forms of exercise. They need to learn how to socialize in ways that don't involve social media—conversation, spending time together, and serving. All of these will take great efforts on our part as mothers, and these efforts need to begin as many years prior to serving as possible.

Several missionaries recently commented on what they wished they had learned prior to their mission and offered this advice:

- Learn to sew (especially sewing on buttons and repairing rips in clothes).
- Learn to wash your clothes, both by hand and in a machine.
- Save more money for the mission.
- Buy a bike, and learn how to repair a bike!
- Learn to cook in small amounts. Be prepared to deal with whatever the cooking supplies in each area are! Every apartment has different equipment, and most are lacking in decent cookware.
- Learn how to read a map.

- Learn how to eat everything! Learn to eat different food. You won't have your mama cooking food for you!

- Learn how to take care of yourself when you are sick! Your mom won't be there to do it for you!

- Learn how to clean and keep things clean.

Self-Mastery

Self-mastery begins at a very young age. Our little ones are taught to dress themselves, brush their teeth, and go to the bathroom by themselves. This transfer of independence needs to continue and is especially critical in the teen years. It's very helpful to look at your children's day, examine what you do for them and what they do for themselves, and consider which responsibilities you can transition completely to them:

- Your children wake up. Do YOU wake them up? Remember, that won't happen in the MTC. It would be helpful to purchase an alarm clock, teach them how it works, and help them take complete responsibility for waking up on time in the morning. It will be a great benefit to them in the mission field.

- Your children eat breakfast. In the mission field, they will make their own. Take the time to teach them a variety of options and how to make them on their own.

- Your children gets dressed every morning. At a very young age, help them learn to pick out their own clothes and be responsible for dressing appropriately according to the situation. As soon as they are able, teach them to wash their own clothes, care for their shoes, and begin learning to mend their clothes.

- Your children participate in scripture study. Obtain a set of scriptures for each child. Teach them to set aside time for personal reading. Help them learn how to mark their scriptures. Teaching this independent habit of scripture study is so important.

- Your children learn to say prayers. Again, begin at an early age to transition this to a personal habit. When they are making tough decisions, remind them to pray. Ask them if they are receiving answers through prayer. Help them learn that they can take personal questions to the Lord, and teach them how to recognize answers.

Look at every aspect of their daily lives. Identify those behaviors that you can teach, and then take steps to transfer responsibility to the child. Teach and transfer, this is the pattern of preparation. "Self-mastery is a challenge for every individual. Only we can control our appetites and passions. Self-mastery cannot be bought by money or fame. It is the ultimate test of our character. It requires climbing out of the deep valleys of our lives and scaling our own Mount Everests. As full-time missionaries we learn great lessons in self-mastery. We learn to get up when we should get up, to work when we should work, and to go to bed when we should go to bed. Full-time missionaries are generally admired and even respected" (James E. Faust, "The Power of Self-Mastery," *Ensign*, May 2000, 43).

One mother helped both of her sons adapt to

Thoughts from a mission president's wife

"GIVE YOUR SONS AND DAUGHTERS a true perspective of what a mission is. It is HARD WORK and LONG DAYS—days full of activities they are not used to. The first two weeks out of the MTC are a difficult adjustment, and some new missionaries are ready to go home after just a few days. But if they can hang in there for two weeks and then stretch it to two months, they will adjust to the schedule and the hard work will become routine. If they are prepared to feel this way and know it is normal, chances might be greater they can push through the first rush of difficult adjustments."

missionary life long before they served. She had her children get up early each day for early morning seminary. For many months before her sons left on their missions, she had them living on a missionary schedule so that the transition was easy. Another friend had "unplugged" times for her family, during which they were not allowed to use electronics of any kind. Restricting screen time will permit our children to learn other ways of reducing stress, spending leisure time, and socializing. Other families limit their children's use of a computer or tablet to a selected amount of time each day. Let the Spirit help you decide how to implement a balanced schedule in the lives of your children so that they will be better prepared for the experience ahead.

Missionary Letter

"I ALSO WASHED my clothes this morning for the first time by hand . . . not fun. I rubbed my hands raw and now they hurt like a rug burn. I have that to look forward to in the future but my hands will get used to it."

Being Prepared Financially

Part of preparing our children to serve missions is teaching them financial preparedness. It is crucial that we have conversations and begin the process of saving as early as is possible. For some this process will start when their children are very young. Others may have only a few years to save. Regardless of the circumstance, it is so important that we teach our children to save for their mission when possible. Making this sacrifice month after month is an incredibly important part of a child's preparation and can reinforce his or her commitment to serve. A former mission president states, "In my experience, missionaries who pay at least part of the cost of their mission are often more dedicated and have fewer concerns about money while in the mission field" (Robert K. Wagstaff, "Preparing Emotionally for Missionary Service," 23).

Part of helping our children in their self-governance is teaching them systems that will help them. There are many, many resources available to help with this. For example, your child may struggle to remember to say his or her prayers. Consider getting a prayer rock to place on his or her pillow at night. Once the child has said a personal prayer, the rock can be moved to the floor, where it will serve as a reminder for morning prayer when the child gets out of bed. Maybe your children struggle with brushing their teeth. Perhaps you could purchase a brightly colored toothbrush to put in plain sight to remind them to brush. You may teach them to use checklists for each day. Teach them to target the habit that needs work and develop a system to help them accomplish this. The same types of reminders and strategies can be used to teach wise financial habits. Help your children remember to save from an early age.

Making the Sacrifice

Every mission involves sacrifice. The scriptures are full of stories of the sacrifices of missionaries. Some of the sons of Mosiah, including Aaron and a number of his fellow missionaries, were cast into prison naked and starved; Alma and Amulek had to watch believing families burned, and Amulek lost everything he had—his family and his possessions; Ammon worked hard for many days for the king before even being able to deliver a single word of his message. Sacrifice is part of serving a mission.

It is always enlightening to describe a mission to a person not of our faith. They start, "So does your church pay your missionaries?"

"Well, no," we reply. "The missionary and usually his or her family pays for the entire mission."

The friend begins to look incredulous. "And it's how long?"

"Two years for young men and a year and a half for young women," we answer.

Their jaw drops. "So can they go to school or work or date?"

We chuckle, "No, they work very hard every day, spreading the gospel and working for the Lord." And the explanation continues: no TV, no movies, no dating, no swimming, no personal electronic usage, no phone calls to home, only weekly email contact or letters, and on and on. Their entire lives are put on hold while they serve the Lord.

"Wow, that's quite a sacrifice," our friend responds.

"Yes it is," we answer. "But our missionaries are willing to sacrifice everything for the Lord because He sacrificed everything for us."

Teaching our children about sacrifice now and the commitment to sacrifice in the future is an integral part of preparing them for their mission.

Our children can also be reassured by the blessings that will come from their sacrifices.

"Is it worth it?" our children may ask.

The Lord provides the answer: "And if it so be that you should labor all your days in crying repentance unto this people, and bring, save it be one soul unto me, how great shall be your joy with him in the kingdom of my Father! And now, if your joy will be great with one soul that you have brought unto me into the kingdom of my Father, how great will be your joy if you should bring many souls unto me!" (D&C 18:15–16). ✳

Share with your children missionary stories from your own family. I shall ever be thankful for the missionaries who found my young mother's family in the deep south back in the early 1920s and baptized her parents. All the great blessings in my life—the gospel, the temple sealing, my very life itself, everything I know and love—have all come as a result of two young missionaries who found my family.

Is it worth it? More than you shall ever know, my child.

Help your children to work hard, to sacrifice, and then to give their gift of service to the Lord and reap blessings throughout eternity.

☀ WHAT THEY NEED TO KNOW:

- Work is good.
- Being prepared with life skills will make them ready to serve the Lord.
- Taking responsibility is the first step toward independence.
- Being prepared for a mission involves mastery of self.
- Serving a mission will require flexibility and the ability to adapt to completely new environments.

TEACH ME ALL THAT I MUST DO

- Going on a mission will require sacrifice.
- Sacrifice brings forth blessings.

⚙ WHAT THEY NEED TO DO:

- Learn to work hard to build stamina.
- Learn and master life skills so they are prepared to take care of themselves as missionaries.
- As they mature, take on more and more self-governance.
- Learn patterns of behavior that will help them adapt to the mission environment.
- Save money for their missions.

♥ WHAT THEY NEED TO BE:

"Behold, I say unto you that it is my will that you should go forth and not tarry, neither be idle but labor with your might—Lifting up your voices as with the sound of a trump, proclaiming the truth according to the revelations and commandments which I have given you" (D&C 75:3–4).

CHAPTER 3

FOCUS ON GOALS AND GROWTH
Emily Freeman, DeAnne Flynn, and Merrilee Boyack

"They were firm, and steadfast, and immovable, willing with all diligence to keep the commandments of the Lord."
3 NEPHI 6:14

From the very minute you hold that newborn child in your arms, you can't help but wonder who he or she will turn out to be. Perhaps it is the depth within the baby's eyes, or maybe it is the tiny fingerprint on the tip of each finger that inspires you to believe that one day that child will be remarkable. And then come the terrible threes, or fifth grade, or a fourteenth birthday. These are some of the hardest years for raising a child. Sometimes during these years we forget how remarkable that child could be. In those moments, *especially those moments,* we need to remember that God has blessed all children with unique gifts and talents that will allow them to reach their potential, and we must not forget what that potential might be.

Helping Children Reach Their Potential

Many children struggle through those formidable years, and there are a couple of hints that may be helpful. One of those hints is to remember what techniques helped you get your child through the three-year-old year. Whatever techniques helped that child learn to calm tantrums and find independence when he or she was three can help again in fifth grade and again at age fourteen. Each child is different, their struggles are different, and because of that, the best techniques during the three-year-old year are different for each one. But one thing is true for all children—the patience and the techniques that help us get them through those pivotal early years will prove beneficial in the coming years when they will struggle again.

Another hint is to remember the potential God sees in our children during those pivotal years. One mother shares this experience:

"I have a daughter who struggled terribly through her fifth-grade year. It was hard for her to see the good in life. In fact, it was hard for all of us to see the good. I found myself focusing on all of the things that weren't going right during that time. Working through those bad habits filled most of our conversations. One day I realized I hadn't noticed anything good about this daughter for several weeks. That afternoon I found her school picture from several years before; it was a time when she had been happy and easy to get along with. Looking at that picture reminded me of some of the gifts I knew she had been blessed with, gifts that had gotten lost under all of the negative traits that we were currently focusing on. One of those gifts was her ability to see a need and to serve without even being asked. I hadn't seen that characteristic in months.

"I hung that picture on the mirror in my bathroom so that every day I would be reminded of that gift she had been given, and an interesting thing happened—our conversations became filled with ways that she could rediscover and use that gift. Instead of focusing on the bad things that were happening, I began focusing on the good things that happened every time she used that gift and every time she reached that potential. Focusing on that gift is what got us through that really hard year. It helped my daughter become the person the Lord needed her to become."

One of our most important roles as mothers is to help our children remember and discover the gifts that they have been given and the potential that God sees in them. Sometimes our children just need a reminder of those gifts to help them become the powerful people they are.

"With all my capacity I encourage you to discover who you really are. I invite you to look beyond the daily routine of life. I urge you to discern through the Spirit your divinely given capacities. I exhort you to prayerfully make worthy choices that will lead you to realize your full potential" (Richard G. Scott, "Realize Your Full Potential," *Ensign,* Nov. 2003, 41).

The book of Moses teaches a powerful reminder of who we are and who we have the capacity to become. In the very beginning of this book, God speaks to Moses and says, "Behold, I am the Lord God Almighty . . . And, behold, thou art my son . . . And I have a work for thee, Moses, my son" (Moses 1:3–4, 6). If the Lord could, I believe He would say that to every one of our children. He knows each son and each daughter. His input is essential, for as He said, "all things are numbered unto me, for they are mine and I know them" (Moses 1:35). He knows our children better than we do; therefore, obtaining His insight is invaluable.

But how do we gain His insight?

We can turn to the scriptures for help. We can study the sections on gifts found in Doctrine and Covenants 46 and in 1 Corinthians 12. Through prayer, inspiration will come. Another place to discover this insight is through our children's patriarchal blessings.

Helping Them Find Their Direction

Most of our children will have the opportunity to receive patriarchal blessings. Each individual blessing mentions the love and careful planning that child completed with his or her Heavenly Father before coming to earth. Each blessing also speaks of special promises, blessings, and gifts to be bestowed *if* the child lives worthy to receive them.

One mother says this of her children's experiences with patriarchal blessings: "When I check in with my fourteen-year-old son at bedtime, he's often reading his patriarchal blessing. This personal 'letter' from a loving Heavenly Father is a real tender mercy for him. I have always believed that if my children are ready, worthy, and willing to enter the holy temple, they can also become ready to receive their patriarchal blessings. So they've all prepared to receive them between twelve to fourteen years old. (Think of Nephi, Mary the Mother of Jesus, David, Samuel, Ishmael,

Ruth, Joseph of Egypt, Joseph Smith, and many others throughout scripture who were all very young when they had dealings with the Lord.) Can you imagine a better time in life to receive a reassuring message from God than when our youth feel the most vulnerable? Remember junior high school? The 'Do I matter? Who am I . . . really? Don't look at me—wait! Please notice me' phase?" The appropriate age to receive a patriarchal blessing will vary for each child, but as mothers we can prepare them for this important step from a young age.

Personalized inspiration and direction from God is invaluable while young people are making key life decisions. President Thomas S. Monson likens this extraordinary guide unto having a personal Liahona and urges every worthy, baptized member to receive a patriarchal blessing (see "Your Patriarchal Blessing: A Liahona of Light," *Ensign,* Nov. 1986, 65–67). Often, important promises in our individual blessings follow the word "if." Help your children deeply appreciate these promises. Highlight them. And commit them to heart. "For he will fulfill all his promises which he shall make unto you" (Alma 37:17) *if* you try to live worthy to receive them.

Richard G. Scott explains, "The Lord is sending more exceptional spirits to earth. As a body they excel the average capacity of their forebears. Their potential for personal growth and positive contribution is enormous. As parents and leaders, how are you cultivating that potential? As a young man or woman of this generation, what are you doing to realize your extraordinary potential? Will you nurture it and rise to exceptional heights of accomplishment and happiness?" ("Realize Your Full Potential," *Ensign,* Nov. 2003, 41).

Establish a Pattern of Setting Goals

Closely related to this subject of helping our children discover their gifts and their potential is the pattern of setting goals and working toward them. Missionaries are taught from day one to set goals. They are given planners, in which they carefully note their goals and their efforts to accomplish them. This is an essential part of being a missionary.

Helping our children learn to set goals at a young age will set up a pattern of successful behavior. There are many ways to do this:

- Consider encouraging your children to set their goals in January. Help them identify specific, measurable goals in a variety of areas—spiritual, physical, academic, etc. Perhaps you will type or write these goals on paper and hang them on the wall by their beds, where they will see them when they wake up. Remember to review their efforts with them all year long.

- Another idea is to have your children set their goals in their journals. Each Sunday they can check their progress and add new goals as needed.

- Church programs provide a great opportunity for learning to set goals. As children enter Cub Scouts and Achievement Days, help them set up charts to track their progress. As your kids progress to Boy Scouts and Personal Progress programs, continue to have them track their progress on their charts or on the computer so that goal-setting and regular review become part of their routine.

- Another idea is to purchase planners for your children and teach them to write down their activities and goals, keep their own calendars, and track their progress in each area.

Many other methods are available and can be found on the internet with a simple search for "children goal setting."

The most important part of this process (and often the hardest!) is to transition so your son or daughter becomes the one setting the goals, working on them, and recording progress. If Mom stays in charge, these behaviors often will not become permanent. President Henry B. Eyring taught an important principle about self-improvement: "Most of us have had some experience with self-improvement efforts. My experience has taught me this about how people and organizations improve: the best place to look is for small changes we could make in things we do often. There is power in steadiness and repetition. And if we can be led by inspiration to choose the right small things to change, consistent obedience will bring great improvement" ("The Lord Will Multiply the Harvest" [an evening with Elder Henry B. Eyring, Feb. 6, 1998], 3).

Persistence is an important trait for a missionary. Persistence can be defined as "the ability to continue toward a worthy goal despite setbacks or obstacles. . . . It's learning to keep at something you may or may not enjoy and to not give up just because it gets difficult" (Laura Padilla-Walker, quoted in Andrea Ludlow Christensen, "Living the Play-Full Life," *BYU Magazine*, Fall 2014, 40).

Part of self-mastery and goal-setting is self-examination. Teaching children to look at themselves and their behavior with honesty and compassion is an important part of their progress. We are ultimately preparing our children to become like Christ. Taking steps in that direction requires some regular self-examination and course correction. We teach our children that repentance is important. However, repentance can only occur when our child has looked at herself or himself and realized a need for change. That first step is key.

A great example of this step comes from one mother's story: "My oldest son had gotten married, and we were looking at the pictures from the wedding. One picture caused the entire family to crack up laughing. Our youngest teenage son had taken a picture of himself smoothing his hair. His brothers were laughing and saying, 'Wow, way to show the ego.'

"Later when my son and I were alone, he said, 'Mom, do you think I have an ego problem?'

"I said to him, 'What do you think? Do *you* think you have a problem?'

"He was quiet and then said, 'Yeah, I do. I think I'm too self-centered.' We then had a wonderful conversation and talked about his strengths and his weaknesses and what he could do to improve them."

Self-reflection is an important part of our children learning to govern themselves and then set a plan to change and improve. We can ask them inviting questions to help with this process:

- What do you think are your strengths?
- How have you improved over the last week/month/year?

- If you could improve one thing about yourself, what would it be?

- What weakness bothers you the most? What steps can you take to address that?

- If you could be anything or do anything, what would that be?

- If you knew you could not fail, what would you do or be?

Patient listening during these discussions can help children learn to look at themselves clearly. Avoid the urge to jump in and add something to their comments, but do encourage them to be both honest and compassionate in the process. Finally, it's important that we help our children understand that the Lord is there to help them in this process of change and to give them great hope that they can reach their full potential.

The *Missionary Preparation Student Manual* states: "Missionaries should not begin their mission with bad habits that have the potential to grow into serious problems. Every person can change and improve. Prospective missionaries who have developed poor diet, hygiene, and physical activity habits can begin now to change their behavior. Self-discipline can be learned at any age, but the process is not always easy. If you master the task before entering missionary service, you will save yourself from much grief and frustration" (90–91).

Preparing our sons and daughters for missions can be an exciting process as we help them recognize the potential God sees in them. Helping them discover their unique gifts should be an ongoing process. Teaching them goal setting and self-reflection will move them toward being prepared missionaries.

WHAT THEY NEED TO KNOW:

- God knows who they are and who they have the potential to become.

- Gifts and attributes can be revealed through patriarchal blessings.

- Setting and working toward goals is part of our development in becoming like Christ.

WHAT THEY NEED TO DO:

- Discover their gifts and develop them.
- Pray to know when it's time to receive a patriarchal blessing.
- Learn to regularly do self-examination in an honest and compassionate way.
- Participate in regularly setting goals and working to achieve them.

 WHAT THEY NEED TO BE:

"That ye may be prepared in all things when I shall send you again to magnify the calling whereunto I have called you, and the mission with which I have commissioned you" (D&C 88:80).

CHAPTER 4

PUTTING FIRST THINGS FIRST
Emily Freeman

"They had been taught to keep the commandments
of God and to walk uprightly before him."
ALMA 53:21

In the final years of preparation before a mission, three important factors come into play: timing, priorities, and balance. Each is equal in importance, and each gains strength from the others. Like a triangle, the combination of these three principles helps the vision of serving a mission begin to take shape.

I once played a game using a long piece of yarn that was tied together at the ends so that it made a giant circle. Our group stood together, shoulder to shoulder around the circle, holding the yarn in our hands. Someone in the group shouted out a shape, and then everyone closed their eyes. While holding the yarn, we tried to move into that shape. Once we felt we had achieved the goal, everyone opened their eyes. It was quite entertaining.

Our most successful attempt happened when someone shouted out "triangle." Immediately we closed our eyes and began to move. Before we got too far, someone in the group called out, "How many of us are there? Everybody number off." We began numbering. There were fifteen. The girl explained that it would be easier to make the triangle if we put five people on each line. Eyes still closed, we numbered off again. When we got to five she stopped us. "Turn in!" she encouraged. "You are the corner." We numbered off five again and made the next corner. Finally, the last five people moved until they made a corner with the first person. Then we opened our eyes. Remarkably, our triangle was almost perfect. It was the only shape we made that was even remotely recognizable. The combination of the imagined plan, the counting off, and the verbal direction allowed the shape to be realized.

Those three lessons can be helpful in this mission preparation process. A mission requires planning, accounting, and direction, just like the three sides of a triangle. The first line of the triangle represents timing; the second, priorities; and the third, balance.

Trusting in the Lord's Timing

In recent years the age guidelines for serving a mission were altered. In October of 2012, President Thomas S. Monson explained: "I am pleased to announce that effective immediately all worthy and able young men who have graduated from high school or its equivalent, regardless of where they live, will have the option of being recommended for missionary service beginning at the age of 18, instead of age 19. *I am not suggesting that all young men will—or should—serve at this earlier age. Rather, based on individual circumstances as well as upon a determination by priesthood leaders, this option is now available.*

"As we have prayerfully pondered the age at which young men may begin their missionary service, we have also given consideration to the age at which a young woman might serve. Today I am pleased to announce that able, worthy young women who have the desire to serve may be recommended for missionary service beginning at age 19, instead of age 21.

"We affirm that missionary work is a priesthood duty—and we encourage all young men who are worthy and who are physically able and mentally capable to respond to the call to serve. Many young women also serve, but they are not under the same mandate to serve as are the young men. We assure the young sisters of the Church, however, that they make a valuable contribution as missionaries, and we welcome their service" ("Welcome to Conference," *Ensign*, Nov. 2012, 4–5; emphasis added).

Note the importance of these words: "I am not suggesting that all young men will—or should—serve at this earlier age. Rather, based on individual circumstances as well as upon a determination by priesthood leaders, this option is now available." Sometimes we forget about that prophetic counsel. While the new minimum age expands the opportunity for service, it should not become a benchmark.

A former mission president and current stake president stated that in the past year, he has seen over eighteen missionaries return home from the field before completing their missions. None of these were due to worthiness issues or spiritual issues. All were due to a variety of reasons having to do with dealing with this dramatic change—they were unable to cope, they couldn't handle the withdrawal from electronics and social life, they suffered from separation anxiety, or they were simply unable to work hard and be in charge of themselves.

It is critical that we prepare our children for the challenging aspects of missionary life. And this cannot be done in only the weeks prior to leaving. In today's world, this preparation has become one of the most important aspects of life.

In order to adapt to the missionary experience, children need to work on self-mastery and maturity. Perhaps the question that needs to be asked before turning in mission papers is not how old they are, but how prepared they are.

Understanding this principle is important.

When we approach this new guideline with that principle in mind, we realize that the "when," the timing of a mission, becomes a crucial element. I love a revelation in the Doctrine and Covenants that was given to Joseph Smith on the bank of the Missouri River at McIlwaine's Bend on August 12, 1831. The Prophet and ten elders were traveling down the Missouri River in canoes, and there was a question of whether they should travel by land or by boat. The Lord's answer is interesting. He told them, "And it mattereth not unto me, after a little, if it so be that they

How do you do it? Repeat every day

fill their mission, whether they go by water or by land; let this be as it is made known unto them according to their judgments hereafter" (D&C 61:22). There is an important lesson here—it wasn't important _how_ they went, what was important was _that_ they went—that they fill their mission. As far as traveling by boat or ship, they got to choose what was best. President Monson made it clear that the same is true of the elders and sisters who are leaving today. The minimum ages are not the required age for being prepared to serve a mission. Sincere prayer and tutoring through the Holy Ghost, combined with advice from priesthood leaders, can help each missionary determine the timing that will be best.

As mothers, we can help each other with this part of the process. We should not assume that just because a boy is eighteen or a girl is nineteen that he or she will be leaving for a mission. Instead, we should respect the process of coming to a personal answer about the timing—an answer that will be in the best interest of that missionary.

With the age lowering, many more sisters have answered the call to serve. This adds another piece to the puzzle. We must keep in mind that some sisters who turn to the Lord in prayer may receive an answer to pursue a different course, including education, work, or marriage. Again, that decision is one that should be made with counsel from priesthood leaders and personal revelation through the Spirit.

We also must keep in mind that there are a variety of ways to serve missions, including service missions, family history missions, and missions close to home. Part of the process of determining the timing will require also determining the best type of mission for each child. Counseling with priesthood leaders about both the needs of the child and the types of service available will help you and your child decide on the best way for him or her to serve Lord.

"If you are a young man wondering whether you ought to fulfill a full-time mission, don't approach that vital decision with your own wisdom alone. Seek the counsel of your parents, your bishop, or stake president. In your prayers ask to have the will of the Lord made known to you. I know that a mission will provide extraordinary blessings for you now and throughout your life. I urge you not to pray to know whether you should go; rather, ask the Lord to guide you in whatever may be necessary to become a worthy, empowered full-time missionary. You will never regret serving a mission, but you most probably will regret not serving if that is your choice" (Richard G. Scott, "Now Is the Time to Serve a Mission," *Ensign,* May 2006, 90).

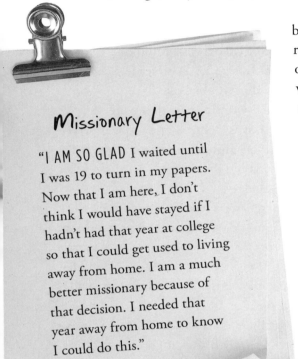

Missionary Letter

"I AM SO GLAD I waited until I was 19 to turn in my papers. Now that I am here, I don't think I would have stayed if I hadn't had that year at college so that I could get used to living away from home. I am a much better missionary because of that decision. I needed that year away from home to know I could do this."

Perhaps we could learn to become less judgmental in this regard and allow these moments of personal revelation to be made without input or criticism from those with an outside perspective. Timing can be so crucial, and the Lord knows best in every circumstance. We must trust Him. We must trust the judgment of the priesthood leaders who are working with our children. And we must trust the personal revelation that comes to our children.

Establishing Priorities

If a mission is not a child's priority during the years that lead up to it, it will be extremely hard for that goal to be realized. Teaching this principle is important, and it is a lesson that must be taught consistently and early.

Many years ago I taught a Sunday School class to a group of sixteen-year-olds. We were discussing the Old Testament, and the subject of that particular lesson was worship. We discussed what it means to worship something. I asked the class, "Who is your king? Is it Jesus Christ or something else? Wherever you spend the most of your time and money, whatever you give the most attention to—that is what you worship."

A boy immediately called out, "So, are you saying football is my king?"

"I don't know," I replied, "Only you know. Who is your king?"

Three years later I listened to that boy give a talk in sacrament meeting before leaving for his mission to Mexico. After the meeting, he came up to me. "Sister Freeman," he said, "do you know why I am going on a mission? Because of that one Sunday School class."

"Which class?" I asked him.

"The one on kings," he replied. "You asked me who my king was. It changed my life. At that time my king was football. I lived, ate, and slept football. I didn't know Jesus Christ at all; I didn't have time to. After that lesson I started reading my scriptures every day. I started saying my prayers. I made seminary a priority. I wanted to make sure Jesus Christ was my king. As I approached my nineteenth birthday I knew I wanted to serve a mission. I am going because of my gratitude for Jesus, for who He is in my life. I will turn twenty while I am gone. I am giving the Lord 10% of my life. It's like my tithe, because He is my king."

This young man was an amazing football player. He was also an amazing missionary. His life has been blessed because he decided to make Jesus Christ his king, and with that choice he adjusted his priorities. That decision at an early age had a profound influence on his life.

We need to help our children develop a relationship with the Savior so that their commitment to Him becomes a priority. They build this relationship by having personal experiences with Him on a regular basis. Praying, scripture study, and serving are three simple ways for them to have a personal experience with the Lord on a daily basis. Try to help your children make these three experiences part of their pattern every day.

It can be helpful to meet with your children on a regular basis to evaluate where they are putting their efforts and spending the majority of their time. In these interactions, we can discuss their priorities and help them identify where their main focus is and where it needs to be.

Missionary Letter

"WE WERE TALKING about how we were representatives of Jesus Christ and how if we truly understood what it meant to be a representative of Jesus Christ we would have no problem obeying the rules, and we would walk around with our heads held high. We opened to this scripture in John 6, when Christ turns to the apostles and says, "Will ye also go away?" And Peter, mighty Peter, says, "Lord, to whom shall we go? thou hast the words of eternal life." Peter knows to whom he needs to look, to whom he needs to go, and where he can turn for peace. It's that simple, and Peter will do it every time. It's like when you can't get up at six thirty—to whom will you go? When you are struggling with your calling, to whom will ye go? When you don't know what to do with your life, to whom will you go? All I can say is this: that in order to be truly happy, go to the Savior as fast as you can. I know that the Savior is Jesus Christ. The Savior is the way! He has given us the way! It is through His doctrine. Go to Christ! As we draw nearer to Him we will be happy. So here is my question for you: to whom shall ye go?"

Finding Balance

The last leg of the triangle includes learning how to balance. This is one of the most important skills we can teach our children. Someone once asked me to share with them the rules of our home. One of those rules is balance. The years during the time when a child is attending high school are some of the hardest years to find balance. These are the years when children often become consumed with a club, a sport, a hobby, a social life, or an identity. Obtaining a talent is not a poor choice. Neither is participating in fun with friends. What is problematic is when a pastime begins to consume the life of a child. Those are the times when we must step in and teach balance.

There is certainly value in helping our children excel in an area of talent. In our family we have had the opportunity to see two of our children continue athletics from high school at the collegiate level. It was a pursuit that required a lot of time during high school. To excel will always require devotion and dedication. A great amount of time will be required to achieve a dream. But it cannot come at the cost of balance.

In our home, balance is a constant topic of conversation. It encompasses everything that has to do with a teenage life—friends, reading, sports, religion, homework, downtime, family time, and hobbies. Our rule is that each category should receive equal attention—not equal minutes in a day, but equal attention. Often when I tell people that, they tell me it can't be done. Actually, for the most part, it can. I realize that it isn't going to work during the two intense weeks of football practice that take place before school starts or during a week of dance competition. Those are exceptions to the rule. The balance rule applies to the days that make up the normal routine of life. Most days should include school, homework, exercise, downtime, a spiritual lift, socialization, and sleep. That is balance.

As a mother I watch over my kids to see that they are filling their days with all of those things. Sometimes a day will go by when they miss one item on that list. One day is okay. But if I begin to notice that for one week straight they haven't exercised at all, it's going to instigate a conversation about balance. That happens because at that point I am not noticing a one-time slip, I am picking up on a pattern.

I like my kids to recognize the imbalance on their own if they can, so I will ask, "Which part of your life seems out of balance right now?" Once they have figured it out, which usually happens fairly quickly, we come up with a solution together. Maybe they haven't had time to exercise because they have been spending too much time gaming. Maybe they have missed personal scripture reading all week because they are exhausted from spending too much time texting with friends. Maybe they are falling behind on their homework because they have spent too much time reading a favorite novel. Usually a lack in one area results from an excess in another. Fixing the balance requires pinpointing both and finding a resolution. It helps if you are vigilant about this. Curbing a gaming habit the first week the family gets a new game, for example, might help to stave off an addiction. Catching a homework neglect the first week of school will help to prevent bad grades.

Of particular importance is helping our children balance their time on the internet and cell phones and tablets. President James E. Faust explained, "In its simplest terms, self-mastery is doing those things we should do and not doing those things we should not do. It requires strength, willpower, and honesty. As the traffic on the communications highway becomes a parking lot, we must depend more and more on our own personal moral filters to separate the good from the bad. Marvelous as it is in many ways, there is something hypnotic about using the Internet. I refer specifically to spending endless time in chat rooms or visiting the pornography sites" ("The Power of Self-Mastery," *Ensign,* May 2000, 44).

Learning balance is so beneficial to a missionary. A missionary's days are filled with balancing exercise, hard work, study, spirituality, and social experiences. It is a great help if their life is driven by those habits long before they leave for their missions.

Sometimes finding balance requires learning to discern what is lacking. The Savior illustrates this principle in the conversation he has with a young man who asks of Him, "What lack I yet?" (Matthew 19:20). The

Savior's reply included asking the young man to adjust his priorities and then to give up his excess. Sadly, the man could not. We must do what we can to not let that be the case with our children.

As our children prepare for their mission experience, perhaps we could help them ask themselves that same question, "What lack I yet?" Is it compassion, patience, the ability to be away from home for a time, accepting the challenge to do hard things, or finding confidence? Could we help them find greater balance by providing them with experiences that would help them become more proficient in the area where they are lacking? Likewise, can we help them learn to give up the excess from their life? Balance is taught. It is acquired. It requires watch care, and readjusting, and prioritizing. It is a trait that, when acquired, becomes a great blessing.

Missionary Letter

"THIS WEEK we have worked the hardest I have ever worked. I have never been this tired before in my whole life. At zone conference the APs took my planner and then they said, 'Has anyone else seen this? He has filled his whole schedule, and he also has a backup plan for every hour of the day.' The mission president told me to keep every hour of the day filled. . . . I just did what he said."

It is the combination of these three topics that helps the goal of a mission begin to become a reality. Let me use one more game example to illustrate this principle. I will never forget the first time I played this game. The facilitator had us gather into groups of ten. We stood in two straight lines, five in each line, facing each other. Then the facilitator handed one yardstick to each group and gave these instructions: "Everyone place one pointer finger under the yardstick. When I say 'go,' lower the yardstick to the ground."

To be honest, I was surprised we were playing the game. How hard could it be? Seriously. The instructions were so simple—*use one finger and lower the yardstick to the ground.* I asked her what the game was called. "Helium yardsticks," she replied. *Weird name,* I thought to myself. Then the facilitator yelled, "GO!"

Now, it is going to be hard for you to imagine this. You might have to try it yourself to believe it's true. Here is what happened—instead of going down, the yardsticks began to rise. "Down!" the group members yelled. "We're trying to go down!" But try as they might, the yardsticks kept going higher. It was as if they had a mind of their own. Honestly, it really was as if they were filled with helium.

The only group that could get the ruler down finally had each member of the group grasp onto the wrist of the person standing next to him or her and push downward. It was hard. It doesn't seem like it should have been, but it was. We all knew the goal we were trying to achieve—to put the yardstick on the ground—but that realization could not take place without completely focusing on timing, priority, and balance.

So it is with a mission. A combined effort in those three areas will help to make the goal of serving a mission a reality.

 ## WHAT THEY NEED TO KNOW:

- Timing requires looking at individual circumstance combined with counsel from priesthood leaders and revelation through the Spirit.
- The timing of when missionaries serve does not matter, so long as they fulfill their mission.
- Making a mission a priority must begin as early as possible.
- Balance is essential.
- Learning balance requires focusing on patterns.

WHAT THEY NEED TO DO:

- Begin now to be prayerful about the timing of a mission.
- Learn to trust and counsel with their priesthood leaders.
- Determine their current priorities, and adjust where needed.

- Evaluate to see what is lacking and what is in excess in their life and then learn to make up the difference to find a better balance.

♥ WHAT THEY NEED TO BE:

"To every thing there is a season, and a time to every purpose under the heaven" (Ecclesiastes 3:1).

FROM THE MISSIONARY HANDBOOK:

"Time is one of the most precious resources Heavenly Father has given you. The period when you are able to serve the Lord with all your time and all your efforts is extremely short. Use it fully and wisely. Such an opportunity is a privilege" ("Missionary Conduct," *Missionary Handbook*, 13).

CHAPTER 5

BEING RESILIENT—
LEARNING TO BOUNCE BACK
Wendy Ulrich

"Neither would they turn aside to the right hand
or to the left . . . but . . . praised God."
ALMA 24:23

As a full-time missionary, I learned what makes a mission hard, and what makes a mission *really* hard.

Teaching the gospel in a new language is hard; being afraid of teaching or of speaking the language is *really* hard. Obeying all the rules is hard; managing internal messages about being lazy and incompetent when you aren't perfect is *really* hard. Being with a companion 24/7 is hard; resolving differences without criticizing or stonewalling is *really* hard. Discerning the Spirit is hard; continuing to trust God when feeling spiritually abandoned is *really* hard.

In other words, the biggest challenges of missionary work are not always missionary work. The biggest challenges are often the emotional demands that accompany constant change, frequent disappointment (including in oneself), periodic loneliness, inevitable personality differences, and niggling feelings of fear or inadequacy.

Helping children prepare for the emotional demands of a mission is not as easy as teaching them to iron a shirt. Their emotional preparation begins with the empathy and support we offer beginning in their infancy. It continues when we both let them fall and help them learn from their errors. It includes modeling through our reactions to failures that feeling inadequate or making a mistake is just part of life.

Some of the skills of resilience that will help youth not only stick with their missions but also find joy in them are emotional self-control, curiosity, persistence, and emotional stability.

Emotional Self-Control

When my kids were toddlers, I wished people came pre-wired with the ability to calm down when they were stirred up and to entertain themselves when bored. And I wasn't thinking only of my kids!

How does the mysterious process of learning not to act like a two-year-old unfold? The starting place is receiving genuine empathy. When we feel understood and valued we learn to understand and value ourselves, and that helps far better than shame, guilt, or criticism—including of ourselves—in slowly developing the skill of emotional self-control.

Some missionaries have more trouble getting moving, while others struggle to calm down. Missions are good places to practice both. Going on a mission means signing up for a demanding job with a relentless pace in an unfamiliar setting, with most of the resources previously used to manage stress (shopping, watching TV, calling friends, playing video games, taking a drive, listening to music) no longer available. It really helps to have already developed at least some skills and resources for managing these demands that don't have to be set aside when the nametag goes on.

Some of the self-regulation skills we need a good start on before leaving home are:

- Slowing the mind and body at the end of a demanding day so as to be able to sleep—without music, TV, or other sleep aids that aren't options for missionaries.

Missionary Letter

"THE BOOKLET *Adjusting to Missionary Life* (LDS.org) is seriously golden. I have studied it so frequently on my mission—for myself, with other sisters, to provide training in district meetings, etc.—that the ideas, counsel, and coping methods are committed to memory. Of course, the book isn't a perfect fit for every missionary, but after over a year of missionary experience, it is so obvious to me who is and who isn't using it. It is a vital step in becoming more fully self-reliant as a missionary. The principles in it are no longer principles in a book; they are part of a stronger, new me, and I know it will bless my life forever."

- Getting up in the morning and engaging the day with good cheer—without depending on someone else to make this happen.

- Being able to identify what we're feeling, keep a sense of humor, reflect on our contribution to problems, take appropriate action to defuse anger or frustration, and help others do the same.

- Calming down when we feel there is too much to do so we can break tasks into manageable bits, make a plan, and carry it out.

- Talking back to internal voices that insist we aren't measuring up and never will and talking to ourselves instead with support, compassion, and encouragement.

- Preparing and eating nutritious meals and exercising regularly to help the brain and body manage moods and energy.

- Training ourselves to scan for positive experiences and emotions (like gratitude, connection, beauty, opportunity, and support) to counteract the brain's natural tendency to scan for threat, unfairness, uncertainty, disappointment, and loss.

Curiosity

Almost every mission has one or two legendary missionaries with a knack for helping people join the Church. I recently spoke with a General Authority who learned about one such missionary in the Ukraine. Curious about what made this missionary so successful, the General Authority arranged to talk with him. The missionary admitted that his "numbers" weren't always the best, but he explained in an unassuming way that he had learned to really listen to people, figure out what mattered to them, show them how the gospel would bless their lives, and stick with them through doubts and struggles.

Being genuinely curious about another human being requires us to set aside our own agendas and self-consciousness and focus on what it really feels like to be in another person's shoes. When we really get curious about how other people think, feel, and behave, conversation gets easier, we can imagine more readily how to be helpful, and we feel the Lord's love for others. Whether or not the other person receives

Missionary Letter

"I THINK the most important thing I'm learning is to tell myself, 'All I have to do now is _____.' When I'm feeling overwhelmed by all the craziness of living in Bulgaria, all the things that don't work, all the things I'm supposed to keep track of, I probably remind myself twenty times a day, 'All I have to do right now is . . . find this bus!' I don't have to speak the language perfectly or teach five discussions or make it for nine more months—not right now. 'All I have to do now is eat lunch.' 'All I have to do now is say hello to that lady.'"

our testimony, each encounter feels more meaningful and genuine to both parties.

Missionaries with the skill of curiosity also apply it to themselves, their companions, the gospel, missionary work, and the workings of the Spirit. Because they ask good questions, they get better answers. They aren't as wrapped up in their own worries, and they are seldom bored.

Learning to be curious about others helps us overcome our natural shyness and insecurity. The most popular training I offered as a mission president's wife was titled "Introverts Can Be Missionaries Too." Most missionaries assume that the One and Only True Missionary is an unbridled extrovert who just *loves* talking to *everyone* and that those not blessed with this skill are doomed to mediocrity and misery. Both introverts and extroverts bring unique skills to the mission. Extroverts often *are* better at fearlessly talking to everyone. Introverts are often better at listening in a way that helps others feel truly heard. Both introverts and extroverts can develop the skill of being genuinely curious about others in ways that lead to authentic conversation, meaningful relationships, and openness to another's life perspective.

As parents, we can model curiosity about why we think the way we do and what the alternatives are. We can think out loud (and with great respect) about the worldview of other people, including those with whom we disagree. We can be curious in a friendly, non-invasive way about our children's and their friends' opinions, experiences, and feelings. We can teach kids directly how to ask good questions and practice good listening.

Persistence Makes the Difference

One of the most influential books I've read is *Mindset,* by Carol Dweck, a Stanford professor interested in how children cope with failure. Dweck gave puzzles to elementary school students and looked at how they responded when the puzzles were easy or hard. Most kids liked the easy puzzles and felt good about themselves when they could solve them. But when the task got hard, many of them looked for someone to blame for their poor performance, made excuses, got headaches, quit trying, or even lied about their performance.

But some didn't. Some children got *more* interested, *more* engaged, showed incredible persistence, asked for harder puzzles, and said things like, "I *knew* this was going to be informative!" Dweck infers, "These kids didn't think they were failing. They thought they were learning."

What made the difference? The first group of kids believed people either have intelligence and talent or they don't. Some of them grew up on a steady diet of praise for being smart or gifted; others believed they just weren't good at school. But in either case, they believed their basic ability was pretty much fixed. If they were successful they felt validated in their smartness; if they failed their confidence plummeted and they tried to hide.

The second group of kids, the resilient ones, had a different belief. They believed the primary factor in making people smart or dumb was practice and persistence. In the face of setback they didn't see failure; they saw information that would help them eventually succeed. They had a "growth mindset"—an understanding that the more you work at something the better you get at it and that ignorance isn't shameful but simply where everyone starts. Their approach was, "This is hard. This is fun!"

Smart, talented kids don't always do well as missionaries. Having things come easily for them has often worked like magic, and when things get hard (and all missions are hard, in one way or another) and the magic "fails," the former superstars don't know what to do next.

We don't do our kids a service by telling them how smart or talented they are. Instead, we can tell them how impressed we are with their persistence, determination, and willingness to risk doing hard things. We can help kids learn that failure isn't the end of the world and that success is more about effort than raw talent. After a perceived failure, asking a child what he or she learned from the experience may be more important than offering reassurance that the child "deserved" success.

We can also teach our children that Christ is our Advocate—the one who is always on our side. In contrast, Satan is called the accuser, "which accused [us] before our God day and night" (Revelation 12:10). When the voice in our heads is accusing, sarcastic, or belittling, it is not the voice of our Advocate. Ever.

Developing Emotional Stability

We sort of expect young missionaries to struggle with obeying rules and taking their missions seriously. Surprisingly, perhaps, many missionaries struggle even more with trying to be perfect. With so many messages about 100% obedience and going home with no regrets, missions can unintentionally influence some people toward obsessive-compulsive tendencies. While some missionaries need reminders to buckle down, other missionaries need to lighten up.

Young people with a tendency toward perfectionism may need to hear:

- Of course do all you can to live the rules, and then don't beat yourself up when you miss one by five minutes. That's why you have common sense.

- Of course you won't speak the language perfectly and will sometimes feel like an idiot. That's why you have a companion.

- Of course you won't measure up on your own to everything that is expected of you as a missionary. That's why you have the Lord.

Another necessary balance is between faith in God and acceptance of reality. Missions can be rife with disappointment. For some, disappointment starts with having to wait to go on a mission or receiving a mission assignment they're not excited about. Others may be disappointed when the gift of tongues doesn't materialize quickly enough, a leadership position goes to someone else, or a beloved investigator doesn't get baptized. There is a balance to be struck between the idea that "if we have enough faith, we'll meet our goals" and realities like others' agency, mission circumstances, and God's purposes.

As parents we can start now to help our children celebrate failure (when it means they were willing to try something new or especially hard), balance hard work with occasional breaks and humor (so they can stick with things better), and serve using their strengths (even if they don't conquer every weakness).

I've never been great at making conversation with people in line at the store, let alone turning those conversations into missionary opportunities.

As a mission president's wife, I wondered how I could possibly teach others how to do something I couldn't do. One day the Spirit seemed to whisper, "Wendy, I didn't call you here for your weaknesses, but for your strengths." I decided to let the missionaries teach me, I patted myself on the back when I jumped in and tried, and I concentrated on what I *could* do well and did it with my whole heart.

Our intent and guiding principle in all our parenting is to help the youth of Zion develop faith in Christ. When our children aren't perfect, aren't happy, aren't great; when they don't serve, or don't finish, or don't care; when they hurt, or struggle, or doubt, or fear—that is when the resilience and good cheer of parents and the love and support of families and ward communities, are most crucial. May all of our children learn from our discipleship to more deeply trust their Advocate, Jesus Christ, the one who is—along with us—always on their side.

WHAT THEY NEED TO KNOW

- Stress is good, and they can manage it and grow from it when they build good coping skills.

- Talent is not just something people are born with. Effort and persistence are paramount.

- The Atonement of Christ can redeem not only sin but also weakness, failure, and disappointment.

WHAT THEY NEED TO DO

- Read and practice the skills in *Adjusting to Missionary Life: Resource Booklet* (available through LDS Church Distribution Centers or at store.lds.org) and "Preparing Emotionally for Missionary Service," by Robert K. Wagstaff (*Ensign,* March 2011, 22–26).

- Stick with hard work by making a plan, having fun, taking breaks, keeping a sense of humor, enjoying a challenge, and sharing the load.

- Break down bigger tasks into manageable chunks and then

remember, "All I have to do right now is _____." If it still feels too hard, break it down more.

- Be genuinely curious about other people, become a good listener, express empathy and kindness, and work through disagreements with good will.

- Learn healthy ways to calm down when upset, talk back to discouragement, and relax and unwind.

- Discuss and record often what they are grateful for, their favorite part of the day, or when they saw God's hand in their lives.

WHAT THEY NEED TO BE

"Fear not, little flock; do good; let earth and hell combine against you, for if ye are built upon my rock, they cannot prevail. Behold, I do not condemn you; go your ways and sin no more; perform with soberness the work which I have commanded you. Look unto me in every thought; doubt not, fear not" (D&C 6:34–36).

CHAPTER 6

BUILDING RELATIONSHIPS AND LEARNING TO SERVE
DeAnne Flynn

"He loveth our souls as well as he loveth our children; therefore, in his mercy he doth visit us by his angels."
ALMA 24:14

My great-uncle Johnny passed away at age 91. He was my mother's dearest uncle. It was a genuine honor and privilege to attend his military funeral. With each successive speaker, I found myself wishing more and more that I had really *known* this man before the last six years of his life. The speakers told of Johnny's close and loving family, of growing up in a home where the gospel had been taught and lived, and of his moving to California, where he had spent most of his long and varied life. Part of the Greatest Generation, Johnny had gone off to war in his youth, chosen a lifestyle outside the boundaries of his upbringing, and had experienced both heartache and happiness along the way. As an 85-year-old widower, my great-uncle Johnny moved into an apartment very close to a remarkably inclusive LDS family, who visited him regularly. They invited him to dinner and to their son's high school football games and brought him audio CDs of the Book of Mormon—since Johnny was blind and missed reading. It wasn't long before a warm and trusting relationship was formed. And since this kind family genuinely cared about Johnny's eternal well-being, they asked if he would like to take the missionary discussions. "After all," they asked, "wasn't your dad the bishop of your ward growing up? Wouldn't you like to brush up on all he taught you?"

Well, without any notice, my mother's beloved uncle called her on the telephone just before his 86th birthday. He said, "Carol Lynn, I have a wonderful idea for my BIG birthday celebration. I'd like you to come to the temple with me!" One can only imagine my mother's unspeakable joy after hearing these words. She had prayed for that moment, fasted for that moment, and longed for that moment for many, many years, and finally, the moment was here! Her father's youngest brother—the last living member of a very close-knit family—was going to the temple, and largely because a seemingly ordinary couple decided to truly love and serve their neighbor.

Oftentimes we have the best intentions of helping others but we're just not sure how or where to begin. We may question if we can really find the time or make a significant difference. Elder Jeffrey R. Holland teaches, "What can one man or woman do? The Master Himself offered an answer. When, prior to His betrayal and Crucifixion, Mary anointed Jesus's head with an expensive burial ointment, Judas Iscariot protested this extravagance and 'murmured against her.' Jesus said: 'Why trouble ye her?' 'She hath wrought a good work. . . . *She hath done what she could.*'" ("Are We Not All Beggars?" *Ensign*, Nov. 2014, 40).

Did you catch that perfectly concise formula? *Just do what you can* and let the Holy Spirit guide. I often wonder if we mothers have a clear understanding of our tremendous power for good. Do we understand that this power starts in our homes, within our families? And that it grows and increases as we strengthen our bonds of love one with another? If we, as purposeful mothers, concentrate our efforts on helping our children learn to first and foremost *serve each other* and to develop *loving, empathetic relationships at home,* it will undoubtedly help them to navigate challenging relationships with mission companions in the future.

Helping Our Children Build Relationships

Teaching our children to always ask, "Lord, is it I?" as they come to us with sibling or friend problems, to show empathy toward others, and to practice the Savior's command to forgive *all* will allow them to more regularly experience the liberating power of unconditional love. We need to raise problem solvers, kids who take personal responsibility for their own words, actions, and emotions. My wise friend's husband, when sending his children on full-time missions, challenges them to find a way to love every single companion. And this counsel is not a surprise to them when they leave for the MTC! The pattern has already been modeled, discussed, and reinforced for many years in my friend's loving home and during their weekly family home evenings.

Since 1915, LDS families have been steadily encouraged to meet together weekly. President Joseph F. Smith pledged, "If the Saints obey this counsel, we promise that great blessings will result. Love at home and obedience to parents will increase. Faith will be developed in the hearts of the youth of Israel, and they will gain power to combat the evil influence and temptations which beset them" (First Presidency Statement, published in *Improvement Era,* June 1915, 733–34). It is important for us, as mothers, to remember that one of the great blessings promised from holding family home evening is an increase of love.

Do we still need these powerful promises today? More than ever before!

When our rambunctious crew was young, my husband and I planned an out-of-the-ordinary family home evening. On a crisp autumn afternoon, as they came home from school, our children were directed to some very official-looking letters in the mailbox. Eagerly, large envelopes for each "Elder" and "Sister" were disbursed. Little eyes grew wide with interest as the children opened their letters one by one. You guessed it—they were all mission calls! Squealing with delight, the kids ran to plug in our electric world globe. After explaining that their missions had already begun, we challenged these newly called missionaries to put on their Sunday best for Mission Prep—*ASAP!*

Our living room was the designated Missionary Training Center, where we practiced teaching the story of Joseph Smith's First Vision. Our home office was the airplane—arranged with rows of chairs and complete with a rolling garden cart filled with pretzels, drinks, and the proverbial ice bucket. And our bedroom was the mission home, where the children were each greeted and given a companion and teaching assignment— along with copies of the Book of Mormon to deliver to the "investigating" families along our street. Needless to say, my husband and I wore many nametags that evening!

With the neighbors all prepped, and the kids all excited, off we went, two by two—except for one "trio" due to a teething toddler. It was certainly a bonding event for our family. And it was also a great way for our neighbors to get to know us, and our faith, a little bit better. Although no one was baptized as a result of our effort, it opened the door to a particularly special relationship with an elderly couple that later became our beloved adopted grandparents. That relationship made every moment of that FHE lesson worthwhile.

I know families who have fed the homeless, visited the lonely, collected donations, secretly shoveled snow, cleaned up yards, shared treats and meals, fixed up houses, hosted missionaries and ward gatherings, helped children in foreign orphanages and schools, and shared their means—both at home and abroad.

There are people who need our help every day—and many of them live in our neighborhoods, in our wards, and in our very own homes.

Texting a loving message of concern, making a phone call or a visit, sharing a meal, sending flowers, chauffeuring, listening, inviting, or doing *anything* the Spirit directs you to do with your children's help will not only bless those you serve—it will bless your entire family as well.

Learning to Serve

President Linda K. Burton observed: "Sometimes we are tempted to serve in a way that we want to serve and not necessarily in the way that is needed at the moment. When Elder Robert D. Hales taught the principle of provident living, he shared the example of buying a gift for his wife. She asked, 'Are you buying this for me or for you?' If we adapt that question to ourselves as we serve and ask, 'Am I doing this for the Savior, or am I doing this for me?' our service will more likely resemble the ministry of the Savior" ("First Observe, Then Serve," *Ensign,* Nov. 2012, 80).

I love the true story of a kindhearted pastor who took a picture of a young missionary while driving through a neighborhood in Georgia. This elder just happened to be mowing someone's lawn in a white shirt and tie. The next time the pastor saw the missionary around town; he stopped and showed him the picture. The pastor told the missionary that this photo was now poster-size and hanging on a wall in his church. Under the picture, there was a thought-provoking question: "What will *you* do to share the gospel with others?"

Are you prepared? Prepared temporally *and* spiritually to serve others? When my friend Katty was young, she lived on a farm in Chile. A sister in her ward was having a real struggle feeding her family, so Katty's father asked his children to go and pick out a chicken for the woman in need. And they did. They chose the smallest, skinniest chicken of them all and declared, "That one, Dad!" With a disappointed look on his face, he knelt beside his young children and

Missionary Letter

"WHEN HURRICANE ALEX HIT, about half of our area suffered severe flood damage. Many people were left homeless from the flooding. The water carried away cars, buses, and entire houses. The worst part, however, is that about half of the city of Monterrey has no water. We have figured out some clever ways to come up with water and the members have been able to help us because they followed the prophet and had food storage. They can serve *us* because *they* were prepared."

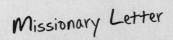

Missionary Letter

"IT'S THE SMALL ACTS of kindness and Christlike love that make all the difference in our lives and in the lives of those around us. Everyone needs someone to care about them, to listen to them, and that's why I love teaching people to pray. When they learn they can talk to Heavenly Father anytime, anywhere, I know they'll never need to feel alone again."

taught them each a powerful lesson. He told them that serving others is just like serving the Savior. Katty's wise father asked, "If Jesus were coming to our house to get some food today, would you give him that chicken?" The children all shook their heads. "Let's try again," he said.

Then, his eager children chose the fattest, most beautiful chicken of them all. The father told his children that throughout their entire lives, they would be asked to sacrifice in order to serve others—and to always share the finest of whatever they've been given. "If we always give the very best, Heavenly Father will be pleased." Now, two generations later, the "parable of the chicken" is still a sacred story to Katty and her growing family. They trust in its powerful message. It also rings true to other parents who earnestly seek to teach that by reaching out to lift the hands that hang down, we all rise up together.

In my estimation, there is no more moving piece of art than Danish master Carl Bloch's exquisite painting *Christ Healing at the Pool of Bethesda*. This touching illustration of John 5, in which Christ heals the paralytic, always stirs something deep within my soul. It seems to strike a familiar chord. Christ's profound compassion, His great empathy for this man who is peering out from beneath the shadows of his covering—perhaps in fear or humiliation—reminds me that we each feel vulnerable at times. Invisible. Scared. Forgotten. We share a deep desire to be whole, to be understood, and to be personally known and cherished. Notably, the

Savior's supreme compassion illustrated in this moving scene isn't manifest in a dramatic, sweeping show. Instead, it is with tender, personal consideration that He invites this man to rise—*to elevate his life* in a single moment after years of low living.

Could "rising up" be that uncomplicated for us today?

Mother Teresa taught: "There is a terrible hunger for love. We all experience that in our lives—the pain, the loneliness. We must have the courage to recognize it. The poor you may have right in your own family. Find them. Love them."

Our children need to understand that we may not know all we can do—but the Lord knows. We may not see all those we can love—but the Lord sees.

May we each *rise up* by recommitting to do what we *can* do and see those we *can* love in the service of our Savior, Jesus Christ. As President Marion G. Romney said, "Service is not something we endure on this earth so we can earn the right to live in the celestial kingdom. Service is the very fiber of which an exalted life in the celestial kingdom is made" (*Ensign,* Nov. 1982, 93).

WHAT THEY NEED TO KNOW:

- Service starts at home through serving our own family members.
- Learning to ask, "Is it I?" will help them become a problem solver in tough relationships.
- Service often requires listening to the Spirit and acting on promptings.
- Serving the poor and needy is important.

WHAT THEY NEED TO DO:

- Learn to love people even when it is hard.
- Serve others by acting on spiritual promptings right away.
- Be willing to sacrifice their best for the Lord.
- Pray to know who—and how—to serve.

♥ **WHAT THEY NEED TO BE**:

"Ye will teach them to walk in the ways of truth and soberness; ye will teach them to love one another, and to serve one another" (Mosiah 4:15).

CHAPTER 7

TEACHING THEM TO TUNE IN TO THE SPIRIT
Emily Freeman

"He has given us a portion of his Spirit."
ALMA 24:8

It wasn't a far walk from his front door. Just a short stroll. But every time he entered that place it was the same—the world disappeared behind him. It was like walking into a secret haven—quiet, peaceful, and secluded. On that spring day he walked to a place he had been to before, the place he had previously designed to go, and knelt down.

What was it that prompted this fourteen-year-old boy to walk into the grove? What did he know? What had he been taught? For some reason this young boy believed that he could speak to God and receive an answer. Why?

Immediately our thoughts turn to James 1:5. That's why the boy went into the grove—because he had read that scripture. But who taught him to turn to the scriptures to find answers? Who taught him to trust the words that were written there? Who was it that taught him to pray?

I can't help but wonder.

Within the wondering my heart turns to Lucy Mack Smith. The

deeper my belief grows in the prophet Joseph Smith, the more I admire his mother.

On that spring day, one boy asked God one question. In that moment everything changed. And then he walked home and told his mother.

A woman who believed in the scriptures.

A woman who believed in prayer.

A woman who believed in God.

Why would she not believe him?

Every time I read the account of the First Vision it has a profound effect on how I want to mother my own children. I want them to hear me speak of my love for the scriptures, and I want them to see me read them. I want them to see me pray. I want them to know that I know answers will come through personal revelation and that I believe they too can speak with God.

But that knowledge can only come through training.

I love the section in the Doctrine and Covenants that was written to John Whitmer. The Lord tells him that He has heard the silent prayer of John's heart and that He will address the subject "which no man knoweth save me and thee alone—For many times you have desired of me to know that which would be of the most worth unto you" (D&C 15:3–4). The Lord acknowledged the question in John's heart and then He answered, "And now, behold, I say unto you, that the thing which will be of the most worth unto you will be to declare repentance unto this people" (D&C 15:6).

Again, one boy asked God one question and received an answer. We must teach our children that the same can be true for them—when they ask God questions, He will send answers.

Teaching Our Children to Pray

This process requires several steps. First, we must teach our children the structure of prayer—addressing Heavenly Father in the name of Jesus Christ. But there is more. We can teach them the importance of gratitude in their prayers. We can teach them a language of respect. We can talk about what it means to pray always, to pray with a sincere heart, to pray with real intent. Instead of solving every question they bring to us, we can turn to Heavenly Father with them in prayer and ask for His help, counsel, and direction. When an answer comes, we can remind them to kneel again in prayer to express gratitude. We can teach them to pray first in every situation. *thank you for my abilities and some fir brooklynn* ⓘ

A third-grade boy was filling out a worksheet in class. The worksheet required filling in a blank with a prepositional phrase. One of the questions said, "The little boy lost his belt. Where should he look?" There were all sorts of phrases to choose from: "under the bed," "in the closet," or "above the TV." The third-grade boy didn't choose any of those answers. Instead he wrote a handwritten response: "Jesus will help you." His immediate choice was to turn to Jesus—first thing. Before he checked anywhere else. How often do we make prayer our first response? *then go looking*

The second step is to teach our children how to live in tune to the Spirit so they can recognize the answers they will receive. Listening to the Holy Ghost is an important part of communicating with Heavenly Father. Romans 8 teaches, "For we know not what we should pray for as we ought: but the Spirit itself maketh intercession for us with groanings which cannot be uttered. And he that searcheth the hearts knoweth what is the mind of the Spirit, because he maketh intercession for the saints according to the will of God. And we know that all things work together for good to them that love God, to them who are the called according to his purpose" (Romans 8:26–28).

The Spirit can help our children know what to pray for and will lead them to know how to proceed so everything can work together for their good. But they need to know how to live so they can hear those promptings.

Living in Tune with the Spirit

Living in tune with the Spirit requires a conscious effort. When seeking an answer or direction, our children can learn what it means to be in tune from Joseph's example. They must put themselves in a place where they can feel peace, a quiet place, a place that is secluded. If they are constantly listening to loud music, talking on the phone, or watching TV, it

61

will be hard for them to receive the answers they are searching for. We live in a world that is noisy. We might need to teach our children to find a previously designed place where they can communicate with the Lord, just as Joseph did. This will require setting down their devices. It might require setting aside time for speaking with the Lord.

Sometimes living in tune with the Spirit requires us to make changes in our lives. The wrong music, TV shows, movies, books, or even

Missionary Letter

"I KNOW that as we do missionary work God blesses us with His Spirit. God gives those who do His work the best tools to do it, and that tool is the Holy Ghost. I know that God knows us and that through the Holy Ghost He can comfort us. We had a district leader share that if we were never uncomfortable there would be no need for a Comforter. So my thought is that we must take a step into the dark, make ourselves uncomfortable in the Lord's work, and we will feel the Spirit and the Holy Ghost will support us. God will send us the best support we need, the Comforter.

"The Spirit is so key to everything in missionary work; without the Spirit we are nothing. The people who do miracles in this world are those that are worthy of the Spirit and listen to it when it prompts them to do something. Our challenge is to be worthy and then to listen."

conversations can chase away the Spirit. Have we taught our children to understand that principle?

Teaching Them to Recognize the Spirit

Another important step is teaching our children how to recognize the whisperings of the Spirit. One of the most frequent questions I hear in my seminary class is, "How do I know if it is the Spirit talking or if it is just me?" It's a good question. The best answer I have found is located in D&C 11, in which we are given six ways to recognize the Spirit: "And now, verily, verily, I say unto thee, put your trust in that Spirit which leadeth to do good—yea, to do justly, to walk humbly, to judge righteously; and this is my Spirit. Verily, verily, I say unto you, I will impart unto you of my Spirit, which shall enlighten your mind, which shall fill your soul with joy; And then shall ye know, or by this shall you know, all things whatsoever you desire of me" (D&C 11:12–14).

Six ways to recognize the Spirit:

- Do good.
- Do justly.
- Walk humbly.
- Judge righteously.
- It will enlighten your mind.
- It will fill your soul with joy.

Those categories help define how the Spirit works. I teach my students that if a thought or inspiration falls into one of those six categories, they should act upon it. But sometimes gaining a full understanding requires a little bit of explanation.

To do good is the easiest and the hardest of these concepts, it seems. That is because we can't help but wonder if every single good thought we have comes from the Spirit. The answer I always give when my seminary students are wondering whether to follow an impression is simple: "Why "not?" If you have had an impression to do good, follow it. Good will come from it.

To do justly requires discernment—the kind of discernment that helps us to recognize good or evil in a situation and act accordingly. We can act in a just manner, or we can act in an unjust manner. Other words to help define acting "justly" include acting helpfully, honestly, charitably, honorably, legally, and virtuously. The Spirit prompts us to act justly.

To walk humbly means to act without pride. Someone who walks humbly would never place his or her own needs above the needs of another. A person who walks humbly is quick to discern the needs of another.

To judge righteously also suggests discernment. This kind of discernment gives us the ability to see good or evil in a person and to choose our associations with that person accordingly. It is important to realize that the Spirit can help us to judge other people righteously, to see the good in them, to view them the way the Savior would, and then to treat them the way He would treat them if He were here.

To enlighten the mind has to do with thoughts, insights, or impressions that come into our minds. This inspiration might enter in as a great idea, perhaps it will come as a warning, or maybe it will settle into our thoughts almost naturally. No matter how it comes, it will light the way, inspire, and illuminate the situation.

To fill the soul with joy is one of my favorite categories. If you feel joy when you ponder on the prompting you have received, it is from the Spirit. If the idea brings you happiness, it is from the Spirit. If your heart feels light, it is from the Spirit.

Learning to understand the way the Spirit speaks takes time and learning. It also takes experience. We must keep in mind that the Spirit speaks in different ways to each of us. Through learning we can come to understand the method by which it speaks to us, and we can help our children learn how it speaks to them. The ability to recognize the whisperings of the Spirit is a gift that must be sought after.

We have had four missionaries leave from our home. One was to speak Croatian, another Spanish, and the other two went on English-speaking missions. Two of our boys were blessed with the gift of tongues when they were set apart. Guess which two? The English-speaking missionaries. I remember thinking what an odd blessing that was when the first missionary was set apart. When I heard the line again as our fourth missionary was set apart, my ears perked up. Important counsel followed the gift. The gift of tongues would enable this missionary to learn the language of the Spirit, which would enable him to be able to speak with others soul to soul.

Sometimes our children wonder how to recognize when the Spirit is communicating with them. We had the opportunity to have a young man come live with us while he was preparing to serve a mission. During one family home evening he asked a sincere question: "How do you know what the Spirit feels like?" I asked each person in the room to explain what it felt like when they were feeling the Spirit. Interestingly, not one person described the same experience. One said it feels warm, another that it brought tears to their eyes, another described a tingling sensation, and one described a feeling of peace.

I looked at the boy and said, "The Spirit knows how to talk to you in your language. It will speak to you in a way that you can feel and recognize. As you learn to look for and recognize that feeling, it will become easier for you to know what the Spirit feels like when it is communicating with you."

Elder Richard G. Scott teaches, "Two indicators that a feeling or prompting comes from God are that it produces peace in your heart and a quiet, warm feeling. As you follow the principles I have discussed, you will be prepared to recognize revelation *at critical times* in your own life" ("How to Obtain Revelation and Inspiration for Your Personal Life," *Ensign,* May 2012, 47; emphasis added).

We must remember that we are raising children in a world that is fraught with complication. There will be critical times in their life when they will have to rely on revelation from the Spirit to see them through. We must teach them how to listen and respond to the promptings of the Spirit. But there is more—we must remind them of the truth that Alma discovered: "The Spirit of the Lord did not fail him" (Alma 4:15). No matter what the circumstance, the Spirit will not fail our children.

May our heart recognize the great responsibility that is ours to teach our children to pray and to receive personal revelation through the Spirit. It is a gift that will accompany them throughout their lives, both as they prepare and as they serve the Lord. Elaine Dalton frequently reminds the audiences she speaks to, "The Holy Ghost is within whispering distance" ("At All Times, in All Things, and in All Places," *Ensign,* May 2008, 118). What a wonderful privilege. What a wonderful gift.

WHAT THEY NEED TO KNOW:

- Personal revelation comes through prayer.
- Personal revelation helps us learn to recognize the Spirit.
- Personal revelation comes when we live in tune.
- Personal revelation is the means through which God speaks to His children.

WHAT THEY NEED TO DO:

- Set aside time to speak with the Lord.
- Find a secluded spot.
- Learn a language of respect.
- Remember gratitude.
- Let prayer become a first response.
- Listen.
- Live in tune with the Spirit.
- Practice responding to spiritual promptings.

♥ WHAT THEY NEED TO BE:

"For behold, again I say unto you that if ye will enter in by the way, and receive the Holy Ghost, it will show unto you all things what ye should do" (2 Nephi 32:5).

FROM THE MISSIONARY HANDBOOK:

"*Receive the Holy Ghost.* Having the right to the constant companionship of the Holy Ghost, a leader seeks to be worthy and ready for the gifts of the Spirit (for example, through prayer and scripture study). A leader strives to recognize and follow the promptings of the Spirit." ("Missionary Leadership," *Missionary Handbook,* 58)

CHAPTER 8

LOVING AND LIVING THE SCRIPTURES
Rosemary Lind

"And now behold, I have somewhat to say concerning the people of Ammon, who, in the beginning, were Lamanites; but by Ammon and his brethren, or rather by the power and word of God, they had been converted unto the Lord."
ALMA 53:10

"And these words, which I command thee this day, shall be in thine heart: And thou shalt teach them diligently unto thy children, and shalt talk of them when thou sittest in thine house, and when thou walkest by the way, and when thou liest down, and when thou risest up" (Deuteronomy 6:6–7).

Hunter, age seven, heard the telephone ring one Sunday at his home and ran to check the caller ID. He didn't realize the call was coming from their ward building, but he saw a name that made him yell excitedly, "Mom! You're going to want to take this—it's Jesus Christ!"

The Savior is so real to Hunter that he didn't find it hard to believe that Jesus was calling. Isn't it thrilling to contemplate raising future missionaries who know that Heavenly Father and the Savior are really this accessible?

Elder Neil L. Andersen taught: "We hold in our arms the rising generation. They come to this earth with important responsibilities and great

[handwritten margin note: Believe long before we see w/ our eyes]

spiritual capacities. We cannot be casual in how we prepare them. Our challenge as parents and teachers is not to *create* a spiritual core in their souls but rather to *fan the flame of their spiritual core* already aglow with the fire of their premortal faith" ("Tell Me the Stories of Jesus," *Ensign,* May 2010, 108; emphasis added).

One of the ways we can fan this flame is by helping our children study and love the scriptures. The members of the Godhead can become as real to our children as the members of their earthly family. "Because I started reading the scriptures daily, I have learned about my Heavenly Father, His Son Jesus Christ, and what I need to do to be like Them. I have learned about the Holy Ghost and how to qualify for His companionship" (Julie B. Beck, "My Soul Delighteth in the Scriptures," *Ensign,* May 2004, 108–9).

We can help our children understand that what is spoken in general conference and written in the *Ensign* by living prophets is also scripture: ✷"And whatsoever they shall speak when moved upon by the Holy Ghost shall be scripture, shall be the will of the Lord, shall be the mind of the Lord, shall be the word of the Lord, shall be the voice of the Lord, and the power of God unto salvation" (D&C 68:4).

As they study the scriptures diligently, our future missionaries will make Heavenly Father's plan of happiness the blueprint for their lives. They will know and live the gospel in a way that it becomes an anchor to their souls.

Establishing the Pattern of Daily Scripture Study

Daily scripture study helps keeps the Spirit in our lives. Having the Spirit with us makes all the difference in the way we look at life and our relationship with our Heavenly Father. The habit of scripture study strengthens future missionaries' faith, helps them resist sin, comforts them in trials, helps them find solutions to their problems, and helps them understand and keep their covenants. It increases obedience and gives them confidence in approaching the Lord. Sister Sheri L. Dew testified: "Some of the clearest promptings I have ever received have come while being immersed in the scriptures. They are a conduit for revelation.

They teach us the language of the Spirit" ("We Are Not Alone," *Ensign,* Nov. 1998, 96).

You are likely a mother who firmly believes all of these things about the scriptures. If you're like the rest of us, though, you know that the BIG challenge is making scripture study happen on a daily basis! Though we firmly believe the principle, many of us find it difficult to round everyone up *every day* for scripture reading, and it sometimes gets neglected.

President Thomas S. Monson said, "We become so caught up in the busyness of our lives. Were we to step back, however, and take a good look at what we're doing, we may find that we have immersed ourselves in the 'thick of thin things.' In other words, too often we spend most of our time taking care of the things which do not really matter much at all in the grand scheme of things, neglecting those more important causes" ("What Have I Done for Someone Today?" *Ensign,* Nov. 2009, 85).

Are there times when you have thought, "It won't hurt if we don't read scriptures tonight," or "Surely the Lord will understand how tired I am," and you neglected getting the family together? There are so many reasons why we don't gather daily—the kids are cross or uncooperative, it's too late, our children aren't listening, we have too many distractions and other activities, no one feels like it, missing just this once won't matter. Surely you have experienced one or more of these excuses.

We know that there are also plenty of times when you feel that way but you find the strength to gather for scripture study anyway. Have you found that you are never, *ever* sorry when you've gotten your family together for scripture study? Our diligence and consistency in studying with our children sets a great example for them. Seeing us delight in the scriptures and find answers to our problems encourages our future missionaries to want to study, too.

Elder David A. Bednar said: "Today if you could ask our adult sons what they remember about family prayer, scripture study, and family home evening, I believe I know how they would answer. They likely would not identify a particular prayer or a specific instance of scripture study or an especially meaningful family home evening lesson as the defining moment in their spiritual development. What they would say they remember is that as a family we were consistent. Sister Bednar and I thought helping our sons understand the content of a particular lesson or a specific scripture was the ultimate outcome. But such a result does not occur each time we study or pray or learn together. The consistency of our intent and work was perhaps the greatest lesson—a lesson we did not fully appreciate at the time" ("More Diligent and Concerned at Home," *Ensign,* Nov. 2009, 19).

So how can we mothers make consistent, effective scripture study happen in our homes?

First, let us keep our eyes on our long-term goal: helping our children become covenant-keeping adults who have developed good habits that will lead them and their families toward eternal life. Next, let us not expect perfection anytime soon! But do let us determine that we will give our best efforts toward our goal. The short-term work toward the long-term goal may at times be difficult, but we are up for the challenge!

Forcing our children to study the scriptures with us usually isn't effective. Many mothers have found that it is better to try incentives. If you are trying to get kids to do something good, there's nothing like a little motivation.

A friend is really good at using incentives to get her kids to do the right things. For example, she tells her children, "I will make you a hot breakfast every day if you will come with a cheerful attitude for scripture study." Or, "If you will study scriptures with us for fifteen minutes, I'll drive you to school." Sometimes she makes a little treat and puts it out on counter to eat *after* scripture study. Another: "If we read the scriptures for ten minutes, we can play a game afterward." Or, "If we read the scriptures Monday through Friday mornings, you can take the car on Friday night." If we pray and give our best effort, the Lord will inspire us with all kinds of good ideas and incentives.

Once most children get into the scriptures, feel the Spirit, and have some good experiences, they become more cooperative. As we help them study and practice the doctrines and see the blessings in their lives, they begin to gain a testimony of gospel principles and the importance of obedience. "If any man will *do his will,* he shall *know of the doctrine,* whether it be of God, or whether I speak of myself" (John 7:17; emphasis added). Some nights our children will even remind *us* that it's time for scriptures!

Using Scriptures to Guide Their Lives

With our help, future missionaries discover ways the scriptures can guide their lives. For example, when family members have decisions to make, we discuss scriptures like these:

"Yea, behold, I will tell you in your mind and in your heart, by the Holy Ghost, which shall come upon you and which shall dwell in your heart" (D&C 8:2).

"But, behold, I say unto you, that you must study it out in your mind; then you must ask me if it be right, and if it is right I will cause that your bosom shall burn within you; therefore, you shall feel that it is right. But if it be not right you shall have no such feelings, but you shall have a stupor of thought that shall cause you to forget the thing which is wrong; therefore, you cannot write that which is sacred save it be given you from me" (D&C 9:8–9).

Perhaps it would be helpful to ponder and pray about topics our future missionaries may need to rely upon in teaching situations, such as the Atonement and how it will apply to them and their mission, being bold and teaching doctrine, and learning the character and attributes of the Godhead, to name a few. We can also arm them with scriptures that will be most helpful. Scriptures used in the manual *Preach My Gospel* and the seminary scripture mastery passages can be studied by the entire family.

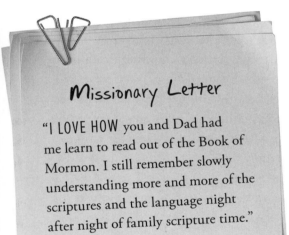

Missionary Letter

"I LOVE HOW you and Dad had me learn to read out of the Book of Mormon. I still remember slowly understanding more and more of the scriptures and the language night after night of family scripture time."

In your study, don't underestimate the youngest members of the family, who always want to participate. Many children hone their reading skills while reading the Book of Mormon with their families.

Having their own set of scriptures will help children engage in scripture study. When children are young you can give them an inexpensive copy of the Book of Mormon and have their name engraved on the front. They can color and mark them and take them to Primary. When children turn eight and are baptized, it is a wonderful time for them to receive an entire set of scriptures, personalized with their name, that they can begin to mark and make notes in. Choose the best timing for your children according to the guidance of the Spirit.

Using Resources to Teach Scripture Study

There are many study aids, such as gospel pictures, marking crayons, scripture stickers, colored pencils, and so on, that can help make studying fun. Many kinds of scripture charts are available. Marking just the scriptures having to do with Christ or other gospel principles is enlightening and can make scripture study feel more exciting. You can start family discussions based on what you read: "What would you do in this scripture situation?" Scripture chases, finding scriptures about a theme, props, costumes, charades, memorizing a scripture together, building with blocks or popsicle sticks, drawing stories as you read, a readers' theater, puppets, Book of Mormon Bingo, making clay figures, and carving bars of soap are fun, too. Small children can draw or work on simple crafts while they listen to the family read scriptures.

Our grandchildren love the scripture stories on LDS.org. They also love to act out scripture stories and engage in role playing. Telling scripture stories at bedtime can create a spiritual experience for our little ones each evening. We reinforce the scripture stories by singing Primary songs before they go to bed. This is a lovely prelude to the children's personal prayers.

Time spent and lessons taught should be brief, simple, enjoyable, and filled with the Spirit. One mother has two rules for scripture study in their home: "Read for time, not length, and be consistent." Her children know there is a designated end point, and any discussion is included in that time frame, so they are willing to be consistent. Family home evening provides time for further discussion as needed.

It is helpful for future missionaries to see how different people in the scriptures dealt with challenges. They can learn from Joseph Smith the importance of listening to the Spirit. They can learn from Moses how to overcome disabilities and weaknesses, such as being slow of speech. They can learn from Daniel the power of faith over fear. And they can learn from Queen Esther the power of fasting with their friends. These and other stories throughout the scriptures can give our children strength and insight.

Are we teaching our children how to find solutions to their problems and comfort in their daily study? They need to learn to look in the scriptures for answers to specific questions. Teach them to approach their scripture reading with a question in mind. By studying the Doctrine and Covenants, they can learn the pattern of a question being answered with an inspired response from the Lord.

Developing Personal Scripture Habits

Critical to the success of our children's scripture study is that it become a personal habit that they are willing to do on a daily basis without reminders from parents. It will take effort to transition from a daily reminder from Mom to a personal and internal daily commitment. Over time and with growing maturity, children will begin to make this a part of their life pattern, and we can help and encourage this process.

Don't forget the wonderful teachings in each of the standard works. Sometimes we concentrate so heavily on the Book of Mormon that we neglect other volumes of scripture. One of our missionaries serving in the Bible belt of the United States wished that our family had spent more time studying the Bible.

When missionaries have paid the price to know the scriptures, the Spirit will bring needed knowledge to their remembrance.

We were pleased when after studying Alma 48:17–18 with the family on a sweet evening with the Spirit present, one of our teenage sons decided that was the scripture passage he wanted for his missionary plaque. Many of our scripture nights were tender like that one, and many others were just nights we studied. Your experiences will be much the same as you find the best time for your family to gather together in daily scripture study. Keep it up!

 President Ezra Taft Benson said, "Let us not treat lightly the great things we have received from the hand of the Lord! His word is one of the most valuable gifts He has given us. I urge you to recommit yourselves to a study of the scriptures. Immerse yourselves in them daily so you will have the power of the Spirit to attend you in

Missionary Letter

"WE WERE TEACHING a Catholic man who asked about the scripture in Matthew 16:18–19 that talks about "upon this rock I will build my church." He asked where this church is today, inferring that it is [not our] church. Remember in Doctrine and Covenants where the Lord says we won't be confounded before men? [D&C 100:5: 'Therefore, verily I say unto you, lift up your voices unto this people; speak the thoughts that I shall put into your hearts, and you shall not be confounded before men;'] Well, amen to that. Because somehow, a very clear response slipped out of my mouth to explain to him something that I hadn't ever really thought that much about before. And to this moment, I can't remember what I said. But the Spirit is real."

your callings. Read them in your families and teach your children to love and treasure them" ("The Power of the Word," *Ensign,* May 1986, 82).

Pray for your children to have the experiences they need to become wonderful missionaries and servants of the Lord. Pray that they will cherish the scriptures. Our Heavenly Father will help you prepare them and help hold them close to you and to Him. The blessings of having your children love the scriptures and use them effectively as they serve missions and continue to live their lives in the Lord's service are worth all the years of study and preparation. This scripture will come to have deep meaning for you and for them: "I have no greater joy than to hear that my children walk in truth" (3 John 1:4).

 WHAT THEY NEED TO KNOW:

- All prophets and scriptures testify of Christ.
- Scripture reading increases faith in Christ and obedience to the principles of the gospel.
- Reading scriptures daily keeps the Spirit in our lives to help us find answers, make decisions, and deal with adversity.

WHAT THEY NEED TO DO:

- Hear the voice of the Lord in the scriptures daily.
- Ponder, pray, and act in faith on what they are learning and feeling in the scriptures.
- Find answers to their questions and problems and teach others how to do the same.
- Be able to share their knowledge and testimony of the scriptures with others.

WHAT THEY NEED TO BE:

"They had waxed strong in the knowledge of the truth; for they were men [and women] of a sound understanding and they had searched the scriptures diligently, that they might know the word of God.

"But this is not all; they had given themselves to much prayer, and fasting; therefore they had the spirit of prophecy, and the spirit of revelation, and when they taught, they taught with power and authority of God" (Alma 17:2–3).

CHAPTER 9

THE COURAGE TO SPEAK
Merrilee Boyack

"And this they did, it being in their view a testimony to God, and also to men, . . . [and] they were firm."
ALMA 24:18–19

Our youngest son, Tanner, enrolled in his high school AP biology class. He reported on the first day that the teacher was a man I had encountered before. This man had attacked me publicly several times for my beliefs. The teacher asked Tanner, "Does your mom know you're in my class?"

"Yes, she does," replied Tanner.

"I'm surprised she's letting you stay here," the teacher responded.

After some time had passed, I asked Tanner how the class was going. "Every day the teacher attacks my beliefs," he answered.

I was horrified. "Do you want me to pull you out of the class?"

"No way, Mom," he replied. "Every day I stand up for what I believe in. And after class, lots of kids come up to me and thank me for saying what they believe but are too scared to say. I can handle it, Mom."

And handle it he did. The teacher was unrelenting the entire semester. At the end of the semester the teacher approached him. "I have to say

I'm impressed that you have been able to defend your opinions," he said. "You're a strong kid."

Standing as a witness for truth and righteousness is a critical element of being a missionary. It is something missionaries do every day, every week, throughout their mission. It is something that all believers do many times in our earthly existence.

Standing as the Lord's witness takes courage in these latter days. President Monson spoke of this in the April 2014 general conference:

"We live in a world where moral values have, in great measure, been tossed aside, where sin is flagrantly on display, and where temptations to stray from the strait and narrow path surround us. . . .

"Inasmuch as the trend in society today is rapidly moving away from the values and principles the Lord has given us, we will almost certainly be called upon to defend that which we believe. Will we have the courage to do so?" ("Be Strong and of a Good Courage," *Ensign,* May 2014, 66).

This is a powerful question for us all—will we have the courage to defend that which we believe?

Teaching Children to Choose to Be Courageous

Teaching our children to choose to be courageous takes time. It also requires that we, as mothers, take a step back. It can be really hard to allow our children to step forward and courageously face challenges, but that transition from being protective mommies over our little ones to cheerleaders from the sidelines is a critical step in preparing our children to speak up with strength and conviction.

I attended a meeting of the school board in which a parent was challenging the school district because he did not want the Pledge of Allegiance to be recited in school with the phrase "under God" included. He was also requesting that the district provide a "God-free" classroom for his child.

The room was packed with hundreds of people and lots of television cameras. I asked a mother in the back how it was going. "Oh, it's going okay," she replied. "I'm surprised at how many people are supporting the guy."

At that point, the clerk called out, "And next, we have a slip from a student, opposed to the request, and not wishing to speak."

The woman's son jerked his head up. "Mom, that's me!" She turned to her son and tried to quiet him, assuring him that they had said he was opposed. He was crestfallen. "I know . . . but, Mom, I really wanted to speak."

Well, I had seen what young people were capable of in other meetings, so I turned to the mother. "He must speak! He absolutely must speak!" His mother submitted another speaker's slip for her son. A short while later, the clerk called that boy's name.

When the boy walked up in front of those hundreds of people and all those cameras, the board president looked at him and asked, "How old are you?"

"I'm twelve years old," he replied. The president said he could speak—and he did!

"I don't understand this at all," he said. "This just isn't right. I have five friends: one is Buddhist, one is Catholic, one is Muslim, one is Jewish, and I'm Mormon. We all get along just fine. Some of us stand for the pledge, some of us don't. Some say 'under God' and some don't. That's okay. We're in America. If you have to have a separate classroom for the atheists, then you'd have to have a separate classroom for the Buddhists and one for the Catholics and one for the Muslims. That isn't right! That isn't the way this country is. We have freedom of religion and we can all worship any way we want. We can all live together peacefully. That's how we do things in America!"

The whole place erupted into a standing ovation for this twelve-year-old boy.

At the end of the meeting, many of the school board members quoted the young man and rejected the proposal.

I was so proud of this boy. He is now faithfully serving a mission for the Church and is a fearless missionary. I was also very proud of his mother, who stepped back and supported her son as he stepped forward and chose to be courageous.

Our children are facing a different world. Belief in Christ is under attack and strong family values are being challenged everywhere we turn. It will take consistent effort as mothers to prepare our children to face this new world. We can share personal experiences of times when family members or friends have courageously stood for truth. In our family, we share the story of my own dear mother, who attended a very large event organized to attack the Mormon faith. She stood in that vast congregation and testified of the truth of the gospel before thousands. This story has strengthened our children in turn. We can inspire our children by reading to them of the prophets and apostles and others throughout the scriptures who have stood firmly in the winds of opposition.

Because we had a family of all sons, the story of Shadrach, Meshach, and Abednego was a favorite. These three valiant young men would only worship their God—even under threat of death. They boldly stated, "If it be so, our God whom we serve is able to deliver us from the burning fiery furnace, and he will deliver us out of thine hand, O king. But if not, be it known unto thee, O king, that we will not serve thy gods, nor worship the golden image which thou hast set up" (Daniel 3:17–18). Our children listened intently as we read to them that these young men "fell down bound into the midst of the burning fiery furnace" (Daniel 3:23). And true to God's faithfulness to stand by us, these three young men were saved because they were true to their faith.

Our prophet and apostles know what our children are facing in their future. President Monson continued, "We will all face fear, experience ridicule, and meet opposition. Let us—all of us—have the courage to defy the consensus, the courage to stand for principle. Courage, not compromise, brings the smile of God's approval" (Be Strong and of a Good Courage," 69). He then quoted from the book of Joshua: "Be strong and of a good courage; be not afraid, neither be thou dismayed: for the Lord thy God is with thee whithersoever thou goest" (Joshua 1:5, 9).

Sometimes we think that merely setting a good example is enough. However, the Lord counseled His people repeatedly in the latter days: "But with some I am not well pleased, for they will not open their mouths, but they hide the talent which I have given unto them, because of the fear of man. Wo unto such, for mine anger is kindled against them.

And it shall come to pass, if they are not more faithful unto me, it shall be taken away, even that which they have" (D&C 60:2–3).

"And at all times, and in all places, he shall open his mouth and declare my gospel as with the voice of a trump, both day and night. And I will give unto him strength such as is not known among men" (D&C 24:12).

Learning to Speak Up

The Lord expects us to open our mouths and speak. Part of our preparing our children to be missionaries is helping them practice speaking up and speaking out. This is no easy task. This practicing begins in the home in the quiet, humble settings of our family home evening and in discussions at family dinners. These times offer a wonderful opportunity for us to have our children teach and testify. Even little ones can speak and grow more comfortable with practice. The Church offers wonderful opportunities from the age of three for our children to practice speaking.

But we must encourage our children to take this one step further and learn to speak up. Their school experiences often provide good opportunities to do this. Our children can write papers that speak to their beliefs. They can give oral reports in the classroom on their values and religious experiences, when appropriate. And they can learn to speak up in social settings to defend truth and righteousness.

As mothers, we must not only encourage our children to speak out but we must model this behavior in our own lives. I was inspired by my own parents, who had many experiences of standing for truth in their lives. I watch my own son, who is very active in politics, inspiring his little ones to fight for liberty. And as we see others do so, it is a great opportunity to point these examples out to our children to teach them the importance of speaking up and opening our mouths in the defense of truth.

In being His witnesses, the counsel of President Hinckley is important: "I am not one to advocate shouting defiantly or shaking fists and issuing threats in the faces of legislators. But I am one who believes that we should earnestly and sincerely and positively express our convictions. . . .

Missionary Letter

"SO THE SUCCESS we had this week, thanks to the Lord, was a miracle. We started contacting in a different colony and met a lot of people. We were in one lesson and this old guy just walks up and enters into the gate to start spitting out all these anti-Mormon things. The lady we were talking with didn't know him—he just came to attack us. So we got up and left because the guy just wanted to contend. We continued contacting and he followed us, so we went up to him and just said, 'Look we can be friends,' and we tried talking about other things than religion, but he kept bringing it up and cussing at us. . . . An old lady walked up and said, 'Elders, come with me to my house.' We followed her and left the guy and talked with her. She has talked with a lot of missionaries, knows the Church is true, and wants to be baptized. Miracle!"

Let our voices be heard. I hope they will not be shrill voices, but I hope we shall speak with such conviction that those to whom we speak shall know of the strength of our feeling and the sincerity of our effort" ("In Opposition to Evil," *Ensign,* Sept. 2004, 5).

How we speak up is important. Certainly there are times when we need to stand and boldly testify. But more often, we will be responding to situations with calm and conviction.

Elder Holland spoke of a similar experience in a recent conference. He told of a young sister missionary being spit upon and pelted with potatoes, and he gave this counsel: "With admiration and encouragement for everyone who will need to remain steadfast in these latter days, I say to all and especially the youth of the Church that if you haven't already, you will one day find yourself called upon to defend your faith or perhaps even endure some personal abuse simply because you are a member of The Church of Jesus Christ of Latter-day Saints. Such moments will require both courage and courtesy on your part" ("The Cost—and Blessings—of Discipleship," *Ensign,* May 2014, 6). Courtesy is a critical element when we are testifying of our convictions. We can teach our children courtesy in their expressions by constant reinforcement at home and in modeling proper responses ourselves.

Courtesy walks hand in hand with love and kindness. Raising four sons, we had many, many family home evenings and daily conversations on kindness and reducing contention. And as I would hear raised voices, I would sing in a loud voice, "Let us oft speak kind words to each other!" (*Hymns* [1985], 232). As mothers, we are constantly teaching our children courtesy, love, and kindness in all that we do and say.

Learning to Bear Testimony

Part of our standing as His witness involves bearing our testimonies and testifying of Christ. This is the language of a missionary. Speaking of our faith in Christ is something we have covenanted to do: "Yea, and are willing to . . . stand as witnesses of God at all times and in all things, and in all places that ye may be in, even until death, that ye may be redeemed of God, and be numbered with those of the first resurrection, that ye may have eternal life" (Mosiah 18:9).

We can encourage our children to bear their testimonies often so that speaking of their belief in and love for the Savior becomes more comfortable for them. This can begin with setting aside time at the end of family home evening to testify of Christ and help even little ones talk of their love for Jesus. As they participate in Primary and grow, invite them to bear their testimonies of Christ often in talks they prepare or comments they give in class or sharing time. Then encourage them to talk of Jesus with their friends and acquaintances and to share those experiences at family dinnertime. Over time, they will gain experience and confidence that will serve them well on their missions.

Responding to Promptings to Speak

Finally, we need to teach our children to respond to promptings that will come to them to stand as His witness. President Gordon B. Hinckley referred to these moments as "days of decision." He states, "There certainly will be days of decision in the lives of each of us. It was ever thus" ("Pursue the Steady Course," *Ensign,* January 2005, 6).

There will be times when the Spirit will prompt our children to speak up and testify. As mothers, we can teach them to learn to identify the promptings of the Holy Ghost and to respond with fearlessness. Each time our children share these experiences with us, we can teach them to take a step back to identify the prompting.

One day I was talking to my son Brennan on the phone. Brennan had

Missionary Letter

"WE TAUGHT a really powerful lesson on the Atonement. We talked about how we are indebted to Christ. When we use the Atonement, that is better than having to pay justice, which we can't. Man, any time I think about what Christ did for us . . . I just can't imagine how. How could anyone do such an unselfish act? Unselfish doesn't even come close to describing what He did. Being on the mission and working for the salvation of others is really hard but wonderful nonetheless. I love working and helping my brothers. . . . I liked the talk from Elder Holland when he said you expect the mission to be easy? Was working for the salvation of others easy for our Savior? We only get to share a little of the experience He felt in the Garden of Gethsemane when doing the will of the Father. Man, I wouldn't want to be anywhere else."

been struggling with his faith and at this point was a young adult who had not attended church for some time. He related an incident in which someone had challenged the Church. "And I just spoke up and totally defended the Church," he said.

"You did?" I queried. "That surprises me."

"Oh, I always defend the Church," he replied.

"Wow," I replied. "That makes me really proud of you, honey. You're responding to the Spirit."

Tying our children's experiences to promptings is an important part of having them realize that the Spirit is guiding their lives. And learning to recognize those promptings and acting on them will prepare them well to serve as valiant missionaries.

We can prepare our children to be fearless missionaries, prepared to stand as His witnesses and boldly testify of Christ at all times and in all places.

As President Hinckley encouraged us, "'Wherefore, be not weary in well-doing, for ye are laying the foundation of a great work. And out of small things proceedeth that which is great. Behold, the Lord requireth the heart and a willing mind (D&C 64:33–34). This is the essence of the matter—'the heart and a willing mind.' . . . I think the Lord would say to us, *Rise, and stand upon thy feet, and speak up for truth and goodness and decency and virtue*'" ("In Opposition to Evil," *Ensign,* Sept. 2004, 5–6; emphasis added).

💡 WHAT THEY NEED TO KNOW:

- Standing as His witness requires courage.

- Standing as His witness requires that we open our mouths.

- Standing as His witness should be done with courtesy and love.

- Standing as His witness is to be done in all places and at all times.

- We will be guided by the Spirit as we choose to stand as His witness.

⚙ WHAT THEY NEED TO DO:

- Choose to be courageous.
- Practice speaking up and speaking out.
- Learn to speak with courtesy and love.
- Bear testimony and speak of Christ.
- Follow promptings in days and moments of decision.

❤ WHAT THEY NEED TO BE:

"But rise, and stand upon thy feet: for I have appeared unto thee for this purpose, to make thee a minister and a witness both of these things which thou hast seen, and of those things in the which I will appear unto thee" (Acts 26:16).

FROM THE MISSIONARY HANDBOOK:

"You have been called to 'invite others to come unto Christ by helping them receive the restored gospel through faith in Jesus Christ and His Atonement, repentance, baptism, receiving the gift of the Holy Ghost, and enduring to the end' (*Preach My Gospel* [2004], 1). How great is your calling!" ("Your Calling," *Missionary Handbook,* 3).

CHAPTER 10

LEARNING GRATITUDE AMONG THE MIRACLES
DeAnne Flynn

"No man can do these miracles . . . except God be with him."
JOHN 3:2

My remarkably brave great-grandparents emigrated from Holland to the United States in 1906. The lifelong ties they once cherished with family and friends in the Netherlands rapidly diminished after their conversion to the restored gospel. Formerly loving relationships, which had seemed fixed and enduring, suddenly became fragile—even hostile. So they prayerfully made the difficult decision to pack up their earthly belongings and three small sons (with a fourth on the way). Then, they courageously set out to begin anew with little more than hope, faith, and the dream of raising up a family unto the Lord—far from the place they had always called home.

Does this story seem miraculous? Extraordinary? Phenomenal? Although similar journeys have been made by God-fearing families throughout history—like Noah's, Moses's, Lot's, Lehi's, and the brother of Jared's—this was an amazing event! Today, most of us don't have to pack up our families and leave in order to live closer to our convictions. Our challenge now is to *stay,* to remain in the world while not being of it.

My valiant Dutch ancestors' daring journey from Holland to Zion is a lot like our own passage from pre-earth life into mortality. After accepting God's eternal plan for His children in our former existence, we left all we knew behind and boldly set out to truly live our convictions—far from the place we called home. Filled with hope, faith, and the dream of raising up a family unto the Lord, we came to this unfamiliar place, leaving behind loved ones and trusting that God would guide each step of our journey. Does this sound amazing? Incredible? Fantastic? Well, actually, it is!

Now that we're here, we'd better understand how "enduring to the end" of this mortal journey requires absolute miracles. And we mothers crave miracles! That's why the inexplicable wonders that most simply call "good fortune" or "luck" or "being in the right place at the right time," we mothers rightly call "miracles." Perhaps, because we ask for them so frequently, we recognize these gifts and blessings for what they truly are.

Recognizing Miracles and Tender Mercies

A miracle could be defined as a very amazing or unusual event, thing, or achievement, which is irrefutably true. But more than six thousand years of Christian wisdom asserts that a miracle is much more than that; it is a *divine* occurrence. Teaching our children that miracles can and do happen is important; however, teaching them *how* to reach for, recognize, and receive miracles is even more essential. And how can we do this?

By talking about miracles, reading about miracles, and studying miracles throughout scripture. Moreover, by fasting for miracles, praying for miracles, and pointing out miracles as they occur, our children will naturally come to plan on them and take great pleasure in watching them unfold.

The Lord's love is often made visible through miracles—and by tender mercies. Exactly what are His tender mercies? Elder David A. Bednar explains, "I have come to better understand that the Lord's tender mercies are the very personal and individualized blessings, strength, protection, assurances, guidance, loving-kindnesses, consolation, support, and spiritual gifts which we receive from and because of and through the Lord Jesus Christ. Truly, the Lord suits 'his mercies according to the conditions of the children of men' (D&C 46:15)" ("The Tender Mercies of the Lord," *Ensign,* May 2005, 99).

I love that last line. Ever so kindly, the Lord reassures us that He tailors every tender mercy to fit our current condition—reminding us that He gives us what we need, when we need it. Do you trust that God will shape His tender mercies to perfectly fill your needs and righteous desires? Do you often testify of that trust? As women who nurture and guide, we simply cannot underestimate the power of testifying.

Missionary Letter

"THE WOMAN I have been writing you about got baptized, which is nothing short of a miracle! She had so many doubts and lots of missionaries had visited her before, but one day we decided it was time. When we got there, the first thing she told me was that she'd had a dream that a sister missionary came to her house to braid her hair and take her to church. After a very spiritual lesson, she committed to baptism! (I'm so glad I know how to braid.) On the morning of her baptism, she asked God that *if* she was supposed to get baptized to please make it rain. There was not a cloud in the sky all day. Then, less than an hour before the service, it mysteriously poured out of nowhere—exactly over her house! She then told God that she couldn't walk her kids to the church if it was pouring, so she asked Him to please stop the water. It stopped within five minutes. She was astonished. So were we. (Our bishop wants to take her to water his crops!) God is so good."

The Lord's promise in Romans 8:28 is a sweet tender mercy of which

I love to testify: "And we know that all things work together for good to them that love God, to them who are the called according to his purpose." Consequently, we mothers can witness to our families by asking, "How many things work together for us?" (All things.) "Work together how?" (For our good—what is right and best for us.) As mothers of future missionaries, we are each "called according to his purpose." When we testify that all things—even the smallest things—work together for our good if we simply love God, our children come to believe and recognize the hand of the Lord in the very details of their lives.

Elder David A. Bednar teaches, "I testify that the tender mercies of the Lord are real and that they do not occur randomly or merely by coincidence. Often, the Lord's timing of His tender mercies helps us to both discern and acknowledge them" ("The Tender Mercies of the Lord," 99).

Our oldest son, Nick, entered the Provo, Utah, MTC on September 9th in preparation for full-time missionary service to Monterrey, Mexico. Packed for warm weather, he studied Spanish diligently for six weeks. When it came time for his district to fly off to Mexico, Nick's visa had still not arrived. So, Elder Flynn was temporarily

Missionary Letter

"WE RECEIVED A MIRACLE REFERRAL right when we needed it most. It definitely came from God. We love this new investigator. When we teach him, the Spirit is so strong. It's a tender mercy, for sure. He plans to get baptized in the ocean this month. We can't wait! 'Have miracles ceased? Behold I say unto you, Nay; neither have angels ceased to minister unto the children of men' (Moroni 7:29). God is aware of His children . . . and He's sending angels to help us find and prepare those who are willing to accept His gospel."

assigned to the Salt Lake City South Mission (incidentally, our home at that time was 100 yards outside the boundaries of this mission). The Church Travel Department assured our son that he should only be "visa waiting" for a few days and to treat this first assignment as he would any other. Work hard. Stay focused. Find sheep. And so he did.

To make a very long story short, Nick finally left for Mexico after four months. He was transferred three times during his extended service in the snowy Salt Lake Valley. (Remember, he packed for warm weather.) We never saw our son, but many of our friends did. They affectionately called these "Nick Sightings." There are so many amazing tender mercies I could share about this visa "misfortune," but when the Lord was finally ready for Elder Nicholas Flynn to leave for Mexico—the morning after baptizing a Spanish-speaking family he and his companion had discovered while tracting in Utah—he left.

When Nick called us from the airport at 5:00 A.M. on a Monday to tell us that he was finally on his way, my "first-born in the wilderness" casually asked me to go to a stop sign near our home. He said there was something waiting just for me. You can only imagine how I felt to see my son's magnetic missionary photo stuck to that stop sign and to realize that he had been so close to our home before calling earlier that morning. Beneath the stop sign was a plastic bag containing my son's white clothing—still wet from the baptism mere hours before. He had just baptized a family who lived in a mission that was one hundred yards from our house! This was part of his mission, a part that he was meant to do. Tender mercy? Miracle? Absolutely.

The Lord has miracles in store for each of our children no matter where they serve—even if it's one hundred yards from home.

Those wet clothes were living proof of God's love for my son and that sweet family. I don't think I've ever been more grateful to do a load of laundry in all my life! I was especially thankful that my missionary son was worthy, that he was willing, and that he was serving *well . . . wherever* he was called to go. "All things work together for good to them that love God" (Romans 8:28).

Learning to Live with Gratitude

Gratitude is a powerful thing, and it is a principle that must go hand in hand with miracles. When we "render all the thanks and praise which (our) whole soul has power to possess," (Mosiah 2:20) we feel pure joy!

Teaching children to be grateful in their early years can be challenging, at best. The "me do it!" stage turns into the "can I have . . . ?" stage, which turns into the "but my friends are all getting/doing/going . . . !" stage, and it usually takes more effort to delay gratification, place limits, and curb entitlement than it does to cave in to them. But every effort to prepare our sons and daughters to live thoughtfully, prudently, and independently will definitely pay off in the long run—especially as they become missionaries. Entitled young men and women tend to have a very rude awakening in the mission field. Miracles and gratitude go hand in hand. I believe we can't sing "Count Your Blessings" (*Hymns*, 241) often enough during our family home evenings! Additionally, low-cost notebooks make great gratitude journals. Writing five things for which we are grateful each day promotes more gratitude, as well as fun conversations around the dinner table. These five things can include the tender mercy moments of our lives—the daily experiences we have to recognize the hand of the Lord.

Teaching gratitude to our children is so important because a sense of entitlement will prevent our children from recognizing miracles. You will remember what happened with the manna in the wilderness—after

Missionary Letter

"MISSIONS ARE MIRACLES. I've witnessed so many lives eternally changed for good here, but the most amazing change has been inside of me. I thought I knew the gospel, and loved the gospel, but I can now honestly say that I know and love my Savior. Coming to know Him more personally has been the greatest gift and miracle of all."

92

a time, the children of Israel expressed resentment instead of gratitude. Once thankful hearts turned hard, they missed the miracle.

Truly, "the tender mercies of the Lord are over all those whom he hath chosen, because of their faith, to make them mighty even unto the power of deliverance" (1 Nephi 1:20). Helping our children learn to trust in God's timing, awareness, and compassion will not only bring about miracles in their lives—it will bring about miracles in ours.

WHAT THEY NEED TO KNOW:

- Miracles are gifts from a loving Heavenly Father.
- Miracles happened long ago, and they still happen today.
- Tender mercies are sweet assurances that God knows each of us personally.
- Tender mercies are not random or coincidental.
- Gratitude helps us be happier and less selfish.
- Gratitude can be shared through words, letters, and actions.

WHAT THEY NEED TO DO:

- Ask for miracles in prayer and when fasting.
- Live worthy to receive miracles and tender mercies.
- Notice God's tender mercies and speak of them often.
- Write in a gratitude journal noting tender mercies, miracles, and the hand of the Lord in their lives.

WHAT THEY NEED TO BE:

"Live in thanksgiving daily, for the many mercies and blessings which he doth bestow" (Alma 34:38).

CHAPTER 11

TEMPLE LIVING AND TEMPLE LOVING
Merrilee Boyack

"And this they did, vouching and covenanting with God."
ALMA 24:18

We were sitting in the San Diego Temple endowment room as our youngest son, Tanner, was receiving his endowment in preparation to serve a mission. Suddenly, I felt my seat begin to wiggle and then to shake. My elderly mother leaned over, "Is your chair shaking?"

"Yes!" I whispered. "We're having an earthquake!"

True to being Californians, we all just rocked and rolled through the session and smiled at Tanner. Afterward we teased him, "Wow, the earth really shook when you received your endowment. Either God is really excited or Satan is really angry!" It was a memorable day.

Part of getting our children ready to serve missions is also preparing them to go to the temple and receive their endowment. It is a momentous occasion for each. Going to the temple to make sacred covenants through the endowment is a day of eternal significance. Preparing for that day is an important part of our children's training and teaching.

Keeping Sacred Covenants

The preparation for that temple experience begins with the steps of making and keeping sacred covenants throughout childhood. It begins with baptism. As we are raising our children in the Church, we carefully teach them the truths of the gospel and of their Savior, Jesus Christ, to prepare them to make the baptismal covenant.

I'm sure in your home you have family home evenings and many dinner discussions on the covenant of baptism. After our children are baptized, it is essential that we keep teaching and training them in the importance of keeping this covenant. This means that we place a significant importance on the sacrament.

Preparing to take the sacrament starts long before the trays are passed. It helps if we approach sacrament meeting with our hearts and heads turned to the Savior. Discussing worshipping our Savior beforehand, arriving early to meetings, sitting reverently rather than chatting, and helping our family focus on the covenants we have made and intend to keep can all help our children prayerfully recommit each week in a meaningful way. We found that if we model this focus, our children tend to follow suit. "Covenants with God help us to know who we really are. They connect us to Him in a personal way through which we come to feel our value in His sight and our place in His kingdom" (Jean A. Stevens, "Covenant Daughters of God," *Ensign,* Nov. 2014, 115).

Covenants are an important part of helping us become like our Heavenly Parents. Sometimes we emphasize to our children that we want them to live so that they will return to their Father in Heaven. But covenants are much more than that. They are also the way that the power of godliness is manifested in our lives. Covenants are the pathway to not only return to but to become *like* our Heavenly Parents.

Teaching our children about the power of covenants in their lives will involve many teaching moments. We must teach and show them that covenants are promises with eternal blessings and that they have the power to transform us into holy beings if we are faithful to them. "As essential and significant as the covenant of baptism is, it is only the beginning—the gate that puts us on the path to eternal life. Ahead on our journey are temple covenants to be made and priesthood ordinances to receive. As Elder David A. Bednar reminds us, 'As we stand in the waters of baptism, we look to the temple.' It is not only in making covenants but also in faithfully keeping these covenants that we are prepared to receive eternal life. That is our hope, our goal, and our joy" ("Covenant Daughters of God," 115).

After baptism, our sons prepare to receive the Aaronic Priesthood. This is a time of great study and learning both for young men and for young women, who need a thorough understanding of the priesthood as well. You might consider using the *Gospel Principles* lesson manual and the *Preach My Gospel* manual for family home evening lessons. These books provide a great foundation for teaching principles related to the priesthood, covenants, and temples. Perhaps you could invite your children to teach family lessons from these inspired manuals. It is important that both boys and girls study the priesthood thoroughly so that they have a foundation of understanding for the doctrines involved in the Lord's covenants.

Preparing to Attend the Temple

There are many ways to help prepare our children to attend the temple. A love of the temple can be developed at a very young age. You might post a picture of a temple prominently in your home. Perhaps your children could keep a picture of a favorite temple in their bedrooms. Let your children see you attend the temple, and talk about how happy it makes you. Schedule trips to visit the temple and tour the area even before your children are old enough to attend. One mother took a picture of her children facing the temple, added the words "I'm going there someday!," and hung it in her home. All of these are helpful and effective in teaching our children to love the temple and look forward to doing temple work.

At the age of twelve, children are permitted to enter the temple to do baptisms for the dead. What a sweet opportunity for our children to begin to do temple work and to enter the House of the Lord. Teaching them beforehand of the importance and seriousness and *joy* of the work will help make this a meaningful experience for them. Talking about the names of those for whom they have performed service as real people and wondering about their lives and how they felt about the work can help make the experience more real to our children. Help them to establish a pattern of consistent temple attendance so that this habit becomes part of their lives. Encourage them to go often, and go with them.

We took our family on a Church History vacation after my oldest son returned from his mission. It was a sweet and tender experience to go to the Nauvoo Temple to do baptisms for the dead with my husband and oldest son baptizing the younger boys and myself. I shared with them how significant the Nauvoo Temple was. I grew up in Detroit, Michigan, and had visited Nauvoo many times. I would stand looking sadly at the large rectangle depression in the ground where the temple had once stood. I bore my testimony to them that day of the amazing miracle of this newly constructed Nauvoo Temple and testified that the wonderful work of the Lord had resumed in this sacred place. Do you have a favorite temple? Have you expressed your love for the temple to your children?

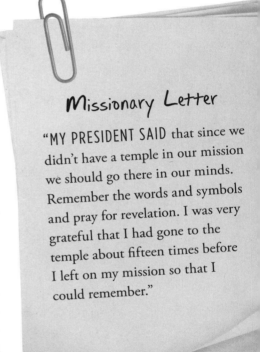

Missionary Letter

"MY PRESIDENT SAID that since we didn't have a temple in our mission we should go there in our minds. Remember the words and symbols and pray for revelation. I was very grateful that I had gone to the temple about fifteen times before I left on my mission so that I could remember."

Temple Attendance and Learning

As our children attend the temple in their youth, we can continue to teach them that the temple is the House of the Lord where we can learn, receive revelation, and make covenants that will help us return to the presence of the Father and the Savior. Having quiet, individual time with your children after they go to the temple will allow you to talk about what they learned there and how they can receive revelation there. Sharing with them our own experiences, as appropriate, will help show them the path to receiving answers to prayers in the sacred House of the Lord.

As our young men reach the age of sixteen, they begin in earnest to prepare to receive the Melchizedek Priesthood. Sometimes families and youth leaders do not give this preparation for the sacred oath and covenant of the Melchizedek Priesthood the separate and intense focus that it deserves. Making this covenant and receiving this ordination is an important and serious step in the life of a young man. It requires significant spiritual preparation. President Kimball states, "Today, the holy Melchizedek Priesthood is given to men who have been brought up as righteous Aaronic Priesthood boys— for the Aaronic Priesthood is to prepare men to become elders and higher authorities in the Melchizedek Priesthood" (in *Conference Report,* Tahiti Area Conference 1976, 21).

A young man will be greatly blessed if he engages in an in-depth

Missionary Letter

"WENT TO THE TEMPLE again today and it was really nice. I love going there to pray. I kind of feel that I can't get through the week without making a trip to get closer to the Lord again.

"We had two temple trips this week, which was awesome. . . . I did almost everything I could do in the temple over this week. Amazing Spirit and learning experience when I go each time. I love the house of the Lord and serving in it this summer was such a blessing! I have a deep love and testimony for the temple and the ordinances that go on inside."

study of the Melchizedek Priesthood. This begins in the Old Testament with a study of the prophets including Melchizedek and Abraham. It continues in Section 84 of the Doctrine and Covenants. Set aside time to assist your son in this endeavor. Encourage him to ask questions and to read the scriptures to gain an understanding of the step he is invited to take.

Many young men will need to go through a repentance process to make sure they are worthy of this priesthood. Speak openly and frankly with your son regarding any behaviors or sins in his life that he needs to repent of. Encourage him to talk to the bishop to review his spiritual standing before the Lord and to personally prepare.

This ordination is a momentous event. Make it a special day for your son in which he realizes the important commitment that he has made and the family celebrates this step in his eternal progression.

As a next step in his or her spiritual progression, we prepare our children to attend the temple for the endowment. It is helpful to teach them about symbols and rituals so that they can better understand the temple experience. There are many helpful resources available, such as the book *The Holy Temple* by Boyd K. Packer and the temple preparation class usually offered at the stake or ward level. It is important to explain the symbolic nature of the temple so that our children can appreciate and be open to this type of learning.

Companion to preparing for the temple is preparing to consecrate one's life to God. Consecration is defined as "to make or declare to be sacred." As our children approach the time to make these sacred covenants in the temple, it is important that we school them in the commitment to consecrate our lives, possessions, and even our time to God. This promise is certainly shown in a missionary's willingness to go and serve a full-time mission for the Lord. But this commitment requires some mental and spiritual preparation so that it is made willingly and with understanding.

"In the long run, offering ourselves for sacred uses might simply mean maintaining a consistent attitude of meek willingness to offer all we are capable of giving at any given time while we help those about us do the same. Consecration seems to be a day-to-day process of dedication, humility, refinement, and purification as we follow the example of the most consecrated person of all time—our Savior and Redeemer Jesus Christ" (Stephen B. Oveson, "Personal Consecration," *Ensign*, Sept. 2005, 46).

Teaching and Living Consecration

Teaching our children about consecration involves teaching them about the little things. We can help them look to the small patterns in their lives to help them make this commitment over and over. Their day begins by awaking and seeing a picture of Jesus or the temple in their bedroom. They say their prayers as they start their day and commit to following the guidance of the Spirit. They begin their day in the name of Jesus Christ. If they are in high school, they attend seminary and learn of the truths and joy of the gospel. They watch their behavior—their dress, their language, their thoughts—to see that they reflect the behavior of a disciple of Christ. They study their scriptures that day to hear the word of the Lord and to have a time when revelation can come to them. They have family prayer and family scripture study to reinforce the entire family's commitment to Christ. They have personal prayer again in the evening, reporting to their Father on how they did that day, repenting and asking for forgiveness and recommitting to obedience. We must make every effort to help our children see that each and every choice is a commitment to consecrate their lives to Him.

"Our life on earth is a stewardship of time and choices granted by our Creator. . . . True success in this life comes in consecrating our lives—that is, our time and choices—to God's purposes (see John 17:1, 4; D&C 19:19). In so doing, we permit Him to raise us to our highest destiny" (D. Todd Christofferson, "Reflections on a Consecrated Life," *Ensign*, Nov. 2010, 16).

As we prayerfully and consistently help prepare our children to make and keep baptismal and priesthood covenants, to consecrate their lives to their Savior, and to make and keep temple covenants, they will be blessed with strength to become like their Savior in ways they may not have comprehended before. We can walk this path beside them and help them to see more clearly how these promises they willingly make bring great eternal blessings in their lives. It is an unending journey of commitment, faithfulness, growth, and empowerment that will lead them to fulfill their ultimate destiny—to become glorified beings like their Redeemer. "Each is a beloved spirit son or daughter of heavenly parents, and, as such, each has a divine nature and destiny" ("The Family: A Proclamation to the World," *Ensign,* Nov. 2010, 129).

WHAT THEY NEED TO KNOW:

- Covenants are eternal promises with blessings.
- Covenants help us to become like our Heavenly Parents.
- The temple is the House of the Lord where we can learn, receive revelation, and make covenants that will help us return to the presence of the Father and the Savior.
- Consecration means making our lives holy and committed to God.

WHAT THEY NEED TO DO:

- Study covenants.
- Prayerfully renew their baptismal covenant weekly through the sacrament.
- Prepare to attend the temple through study and obedience.
- Study, receive, and magnify priesthood for young men.
- Study, sustain, and access priesthood power for young women.
- Attend the temple to perform baptisms for the dead at age twelve if possible, and make it a consistent habit.
- Make a commitment to consecrate themselves to the Lord and His kingdom.

WHAT THEY NEED TO BE:

"And we ask thee, Holy Father, that thy servants may go forth from this house armed with thy power, and that thy name may be upon them, and thy glory be round about them, and thine angels have charge over them; and from this place they may bear exceedingly great and glorious tidings, in truth, unto the ends of the earth, that they may know that this is thy work, and that thou hast put forth thy hand, to fulfil that which thou hast spoken by the mouths of the prophets, concerning the last days" (D&C 109:22–23).

CHAPTER 12

WALKING THE PATH OF CONVERSION
Leslie Oswald

*"And as sure as the Lord liveth, so sure as many as believed . . .
and were converted unto the Lord, never did fall away."*
ALMA 23:6

As we welcomed one elder to our mission, I was immediately struck by the differences in our lives. He came from Tonga, and he described to me what they did to provide food for their families. The men would get in canoes and take big clubs and set out to hunt for sharks. When one came close to the canoe, they would kill the shark by hitting it over the head with their club. They were grateful to return home with food for their family. My first comment was, "Suppose you are not as successful when you club the shark as you hope to be?"

He simply said: "Then you die! That is why on hunting days the women stay in the huts being completely silent and praying for the safe return of their men."

I pictured myself pushing a shopping cart down the wide aisles of a supermarket and being able to choose from neatly stacked food items as I decided what to take home to feed my family. I felt that he and I lived in such different worlds. We simply did not have much in common. Then he said something that caused me to quickly realize that we did indeed have much in common—that our hearts were knit together in unity. As this missionary embarked upon his mission, he said, "If I can obey like Nephi, pray like Enos, teach like Alma, and endure like Abinadi, then I will be the missionary my Heavenly Father wants me to be." I was immediately impressed that he did not say "I will be the missionary that *I* want to be." He desired to be the missionary that his Heavenly Father wanted him to be.

I love the Book of Mormon. One reason is that I have incorporated into my life what we are told in 1 Nephi 19:23: "I did liken all scriptures unto us, that it might be for our profit and learning." In our family we would choose someone from the scriptures and find ways to be like him or her. In family home evening we would choose someone we saw as a hero and then write on a sheet of paper, "Things I will do to be like _____" (whichever hero we had chosen). As a family we were strengthened as we consciously tried to be like that person—and it was always for our profit and learning. Likening the scriptures was an integral part of the process of helping our children to become converted.

We have two sons. The first loved school, and the second could not even relate to that idea. Our second son was not fond of reading. So one night as we were reading the scriptures, this son exclaimed: "That's it? That's all we have to do?" Well, the question itself was intriguing, but even more so was his excitement about something we were reading. So I paused to see what had attracted his attention. The scripture we had read was Alma 48:17: "Yea, verily, verily I say unto you, if all men had been, and were, and ever would be, like unto Moroni, behold, the very powers of hell would have been shaken forever; yea, the devil would never have power over the hearts of the children of men."

I could see why that scripture would be appealing to a young boy. Who would not want that kind of protection against the devil? So we looked on the left column of that page, which contains a description of what Moroni was like. He was "a strong and mighty man," his "soul did joy in the liberty and the freedom of his country," his "heart did swell with thanksgiving to his God, for the many privileges and blessings which he bestowed upon his people," he "did labor exceedingly for the welfare and safety of his people," he was "firm in the faith of Christ" (Alma 48:11–13). This was a man who was converted. What a great opportunity for a young boy to consider the characteristics of Moroni and try to do things to be like him, knowing that such efforts brought with them a comforting promise.

Becoming Converted

Every missionary's first convert should be him- or herself. Missionaries must come to know for themselves that Jesus Christ is the Savior of the world. As we liken the scriptures unto ourselves, we feel a confirmation of their truth and we experience the joy that can come into our lives as we do those things our Savior would have us do. The steps of likening, confirming truth, and experiencing joy are all part of the conversion process.

When my husband was a mission president, we were blessed to be able to take all six of our children with us. Every meeting with the missionaries was a great blessing to them. On the last night of our missionaries' time in the mission, we had a special testimony meeting with them. At one departure testimony meeting, a young man we felt had been a good missionary stood and tearfully said, "I have not been a full-time servant of Jesus Christ every day of my mission." He felt sorrow for the days he wished he would have served more valiantly. At that same meeting, another missionary stood and said, "I have been a full-time servant of Jesus Christ every day of my mission, and I can't wait to go home and tell my parents." My thoughts turned to his Heavenly Parents and what his valiant service meant to them.

My two boys were greatly blessed by what they saw in that departure meeting. When they left for their missions, they did not want one day to pass that they could not say, "I have done what I needed to do to be a full-time servant of Jesus Christ." It was a motivation to them to do the best they could each day—to serve valiantly.

Living Valiantly

Our mission scripture was Alma 53:20, which describes missionaries who were exceedingly valiant for courage and also for strength and activity, who were true at all times in whatsoever thing they were entrusted. Courage, strength, and activity—these come by learning to talk comfortably with strangers, doing things when we don't feel like doing them, and continuing on when we feel tempted to give up. We would hold devotionals that missionaries could attend if they brought an investigator. At one devotional, all the missionaries were impressed with a missionary who had brought eleven investigators. He was asked, "How did you do that?"

His reply: "I invited thirty-three!"

He knew what it meant to have courage, strength, and activity—he knew what it meant to be *exceedingly* valiant!

When missionaries arrived in our mission, we would talk about being a full-time servant of Jesus Christ every day of their mission. Would that be easy? Certainly it would be a great challenge. Just as certainly, measuring up to that challenge would bring great rewards. It is a blessing and an advantage to missionaries to have learned one thing about themselves: *I can do hard things.* Accomplishing something outside of their comfort zone builds this belief within them. Opportunities to do so should be provided often, and acknowledgement of the strength they have gained through these experiences will help them find joy in doing whatever they are asked to do, knowing the Lord will help them accomplish what has been asked of them.

Becoming converted and serving valiantly are characteristics of someone who knows and loves Jesus Christ. Our valiance becomes a witness of our desire to be like Christ. Chapter 6 of *Preach My Gospel* identifies Christlike attributes. "Christlike attributes are gifts from God. . . . Ask your Heavenly Father to bless you with these attributes; you cannot develop them without His help" (*Preach My Gospel: A Guide to Missionary Service* [2004], 115). Christ has set the perfect example for us, and He commands us to become like Him. The attributes described in *Preach My Gospel* include faith in Jesus Christ, hope, charity and love, virtue, knowledge, patience, humility, diligence, and obedience. As mothers, we will have countless opportunities to teach each of these attributes to our children and to praise them when we see them exhibiting these attributes.

Developing Christlike Attributes

I know of a missionary who chose to concentrate on one Christlike characteristic each transfer. He identified the characteristic and pondered how he could exemplify that characteristic in his life. In so doing, he felt he came closer to his Savior every day. In our own families, just as we can try to become like our heroes in the scriptures, we can become more Christlike each day by striving to make these attributes a part of our character. Developing these attributes will help missionaries to serve as Christ would serve.

The Attribute of Hope

In a letter from a missionary grandson we saw how he was able to offer the Christlike characteristic of hope as he reached out to someone to encourage and strengthen her:

"One investigator family just came back from Hawaii so we scheduled an appointment to come by. The wife called and cancelled the appointment due to a surprise soccer practice, but on the phone she sounded really sick. She has seizures pretty badly. So we felt prompted to stop by. She was really bad. She was having a seizure every five minutes and was really stressed and frustrated. My mom also has seizures so I was able to relate to her and convince her to let us help her. She started to cry and said, 'I really need help, I really need help.' So we told her we were going to change and come right back. We spent three hours cleaning her house and just helping her catch up with everything. Her seizures are stress-induced, I think, so we were able to start making her laugh and feel comfortable. They went from every five minutes to every thirty minutes. Then when we had to go I asked her if we could come by later that night and give her a priesthood blessing. She said of course. We went home and changed and came back over with a member and gave her a priesthood blessing. The Spirit was very strong in the room. Since the priesthood blessing three days ago, she has not had a seizure! Her faith was unbelievable. She truly believed that this could help her, and it did. Such a tender mercy from the Lord."

The Attribute of Love and Charity

I will never forget these emails that came in the middle of the week from another of our grandsons. He was given an opportunity to email home because of the unexpected death of his companion's father. The first email is a beautiful example of Christlike love and charity during times of adversity. The second letter is an even more powerful example. I love that this missionary was willing to do whatever he could to help his companion—even if it meant giving up his preparation day. As you read each example, consider how this missionary's actions reflected Jesus Christ.

The Attribute of Diligence and Obedience

This is another favorite letter from a grandson. This missionary could easily have chosen rest and recuperation, but instead he chose the Christlike attribute of diligence because of his concern for a missionary who had only been in the field for three days.

"So on Friday, my third day with my new companion, we were biking to this stop sign and there was a car stopped looking for a gap. The road was really busy. All of a sudden the lady pulls out and hits me with her Cadillac. I got stabbed by my bike handle bars and hurt my knee pretty bad. All those movies where the people just jump up after getting hit by a car are not true . . . not even close. The person might be able to get themselves out of the road, but they will be rolling in the grass for at least five minutes before they get up. The police came as well as an ambulance and a fire truck. Yes, I got a fire truck. But anyway, there were many miracles that came from this story. The first is that the woman that hit me now has a mormon.org card with the missionaries' number on it. The second is that my new companion, because it was only his third day in the mission field, was a little stressed that his trainer just got hit by a car. We went back to the apartment so I could change my clothes and wash off all of the blood. I knew that the only way to help him would be to go out and work hard. So my knee was hurting a little bit, but I said let's go out and I was

Missionary Letter

"HOPE ALL IS WELL, just a five-minute email because it isn't really my P-day, but things are all messed up. Today I had an experience I'll never forget. Riding back in the car was tough. He had just found out about his dad. I've never experienced anything like that. I didn't know how to comfort him or help. I felt completely inadequate. Then I remembered Alma 7:11–12, 'And he shall go forth, suffering pains and afflictions and temptations of every kind; and this that the word might be fulfilled which saith he will take upon him the pains and the sicknesses of his people. And he will take upon him death, that he may loose the bands of death which bind his people; and he will take upon him their infirmities, that his bowels may be filled with mercy, according to the flesh, that he may know according to the flesh how to succor his people according to their infirmities.'

"I didn't know how he was feeling, but someone did. I'm so grateful for the Atonement, for the comfort that we can receive when we feel like no one knows how it feels, how much it hurts, or why this had to happen. I felt for the first time in my life what it feels like to comfort those who stand in need of comfort, mourn with those that mourn, and lift the burden of someone who desperately needed it. The knowledge we have of the plan of salvation, the Atonement of Jesus Christ, and the simple statement "families can be together forever" took on an entirely new meaning. How great is our message?"

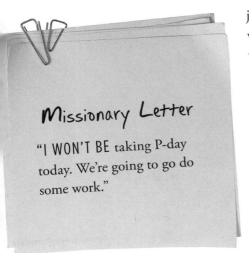

Missionary Letter

"I WON'T BE taking P-day today. We're going to go do some work."

just praying the whole time that the Lord would take care of my knee so I could keep working and help my companion out. It was way cool, because as soon as we got around the corner from our apartment, my knee and stomach stopped hurting. That was a miracle of the Lord. And then I remembered that in my setting apart the stake president blessed me that I would be able to work *every day* on my mission, and I knew that the Lord would take care of me and I would be able to keep going and keep working."

The Attribute of Faith in Christ and Humility

This is the story of one of the missionaries who served with us in the California Ventura Mission.

"I have been waiting for your phone call."

Those were the first words out of the bishop's mouth after my husband introduced himself as the president of the mission where one of the bishop's ward members was currently serving. It had been a month since the elder had arrived in our mission. This missionary was big and awkward and had some trouble mingling with the other missionaries. Several days after assigning him to his first companion, my husband received a distress call. "Help! My companion has already had two bike accidents. If we don't do something, he won't live until Saturday."

So my husband quickly made a phone call to the young man's bishop. The bishop told my husband that he had spent sixteen months agonizing over whether or not to send in this young man's mission papers. This boy came from the backwoods of West Virginia. No running water. No indoor plumbing. The boy's father was an alcoholic, and the family could only attend church if someone picked them up. But the boy really wanted to be a missionary. The bishop told my husband of the countless hours this elder had spent off by himself in the woods reading the scriptures. It was his love of the scriptures and the Lord that convinced the bishop to send him. My husband explained about the two bike accidents and the bishop replied, "It doesn't surprise me. He probably has never ridden a bike before."

We were so impressed by this elder's commitment and his faith. Where other missionaries complained about having to be in a bike area without an air-conditioned car, this elder didn't say a word. When my husband assigned him to a bike area he could have easily explained that he didn't know how to ride a bike, but he didn't. He had faith. He believed that Heavenly Father would help him accomplish anything his mission president asked him to do.

Here is a principle we have discovered as we have served at the Provo Missionary Training Center: when becoming converted, serving valiantly, and developing the attributes of Christ are a part of life in the years *before* missionary service, they prepare the missionary to enter the MTC eagerly, grateful for the opportunity to be a full-time servant of Jesus Christ.

A favorite memory of mine is a missionary who arrived from the airport on the bus. He jumped down the bus stairs with a huge smile on his face. He showed obvious enthusiasm and excitement about being a missionary. He shared with me the process that he had gone through that brought him to us. His father was not an active member of the Church, and he had spent most Sundays hunting and doing other things with his father. He said he was sure that when he spoke in sacrament before leaving for his mission, the people attending that meeting were wondering who he was. He wasn't all that sure about serving a mission but decided he would go to the MTC, and if he felt good about his experience there he would continue on. If he did not, he would go home. He liked his experience at the MTC. But he yearned for a confirmation from the Lord that this is what he should do. On his last night in the MTC he was determined to stay on his knees until he felt a confirmation about his decision to serve a mission. One by one all of the other missionaries in his room finished praying and got into bed. He thought if he stayed much longer on his knees they would wonder what was wrong with him. So he crawled into bed and continued to pray. He prayed for a long time, and still no confirmation. He felt prompted to thank God for the blessings in his life. As he continued this prayer of gratitude, he was overwhelmed with a most powerful confirmation that he indeed was where his Heavenly Father wanted him to be. This is why the next day he was gleefully jumping off a bus.

I asked him what got him on his mission and to the MTC in the first place. He said, "My mother prayed me here." I could feel the love and respect he felt for his good mother. I told him he needed to write her and tell her how blessed he was because of her relationship with him and her prayers in his behalf. Some weeks later when I saw him again, I asked if he had written that letter to his mother. He replied, "Oh yes, and she must have read it in stake conference because I keep getting letters from people telling me how marvelous that letter was!" He did not doubt his mother knew it (see Alma 56:48).

Never underestimate your power as a mother. Your teaching will be invaluable; your prayers will make a difference. Your example can help your child become converted, live valiantly, and learn to develop Christlike attributes. Your child will come to know Jesus Christ through you.

 WHAT THEY NEED TO KNOW:

- The scriptures can be a powerful tool in the conversion process.
- Exceeding valiance will lead to great rewards.
- They can do hard things.
- Developing Christlike attributes will help them serve like the Savior.

WHAT THEY NEED TO DO:

- Read the scriptures and learn from the heroes therein.
- Learn how to live valiantly and do hard things.
- Develop Christlike attributes:
  - Faith in Jesus Christ
  - Hope

- Charity and love
- Virtue
- Knowledge
- Patience
- Humility
- Diligence
- Obedience.

WHAT THEY NEED TO BE:

"God anointed Jesus of Nazareth with the Holy Ghost and with power: who went about doing good, . . . for God was with him. And we are witnesses of all things which he did. . . . And He commanded us to preach unto the people, and to testify that it is he" (Acts 10:38–39, 42).

CHAPTER 13

THE BLESSINGS OF SACRIFICE
Emily Freeman

"They had been taught by their mothers,
that if they did not doubt, God would deliver them."
ALMA 56:47

The final part of preparing your missionary to serve requires a preparation of the heart—*your* heart. After the training up comes the letting go. You are probably beginning to realize that it's not just the child who sacrifices eighteen months to two years of life; in a small way the mother does, also. This is a journey of sacrifice, and perhaps there is no story better to learn of sacrifice from than the one that took place on the road to Moriah.

As I find myself imagining the journey that took place on the road to Moriah, I ponder the thoughts that must have filled Abraham's heavy heart. "Take now thy son, thine only son Isaac, whom thou lovest" (Genesis 22:2). I imagine the sun, rising early that morning. The gathering of the wood. The planning for the journey ahead.

I think of the three-day journey and the thoughts that must have filled Abraham's heart every time he lifted his eyes to see the place afar off. I imagine the last stretch of that journey, as Abraham climbed the mountain with his son—his only son, whom he loved. And I picture him arriving at the place God had told him of and building the altar, somberly, with his own hands. Putting each stone in place. I imagine him carefully laying out the wood, each piece in order. It is beyond my capacity to understand what he must have felt as he gently bound his trusting, obedient son and then laid him on the altar upon the wood.

The moment that Abraham stretched forth his hand, an angel called unto him—in the very moment when it became clear that Abraham would not withhold anything from the Lord. When asked why God commanded Abraham to sacrifice Isaac, President Hugh B. Brown suggested it was because "Abraham needed to learn something about Abraham" (in Truman G. Madsen, *The Highest in Us* [1978], 49).

Abraham's sacrifice led him to discover something about himself. We may find ourselves asking, *what is it I need to learn about myself? What am I willing to give to the Lord to learn that lesson? What am I willing to sacrifice?*

Susan W. Tanner, former Young Women general president, expressed her thoughts this way: "Each time I walk with Abraham and Isaac on the road to Mount Moriah, I weep, knowing that Abraham does not know that there will be an angel and a ram in the thicket at the end of the journey. We are each in the middle of our earthly path, and we don't know the rest of our own stories. But we, as Abraham, are blessed with miracles" ("My Soul Delighteth in the Things of the Lord," *Ensign,* May 2008, 82–83).

As Abraham and Isaac prepared to leave Mount Moriah, the angel called unto Abraham a second time, saying, "Because thou hast done this thing, and hast not withheld thy son, thine only son: That in blessing I will bless thee, and in multiplying I will multiply thy seed as the stars of the heaven, and as the sand which is upon the sea shore; . . . because thou hast obeyed my voice" (Genesis 22:16–18).

In the Mount Moriah moments of our lives, those times when we choose to withhold nothing from the Lord, the times of greatest sacrifice, perhaps we could try to remember that in His own way, and in His own time, the Lord will provide the angel and the ram in the thicket. When all is said and done, He will withhold nothing from us. In blessing, He will bless us.

In those final days and hours before a missionary leaves, every mother begins to reflect on the sacrifice. I won't forget the night before my second son left for his mission. We had zipped up the luggage and left it by the door, said the last goodbyes to family and well-wishers, and talked about the plans for the next day. Then we climbed in bed. I will admit I slept peacefully until almost four in the morning. Then I heard someone awake in the kitchen. It was Josh, my almost missionary. He is diabetic, and a quick poke to the finger revealed that his blood sugar was dangerously low. I poured him a bowl of cereal and sat up with him while he ate the whole thing. Once he had finished I checked him again to make sure his levels were good before sending him back to bed. Then I climbed into bed and sobbed. Who was going to wake up with Josh at four in the morning and make sure he was okay? Who was going to sit up with him and make sure he ate the whole bowl of cereal? Who would provide the watchcare? I prayed for good companions. I prayed for his protection. I prayed the Lord would be with him every step of the way.

And then, the next day, I took my son, my second son, Joshua, whom I love, and I dropped him off at the MTC. In that moment I knew in a small way what it was to sacrifice—to hold back nothing from the Lord.

Sometime in the future you will stand next to the car and watch your son or daughter walk away with luggage in tow, into the journey ahead. Perhaps in that moment you will remember this: even though you know not what the next months and years will bring, you can be certain that the Lord will provide an angel and a ram in the thicket right when they are needed on this journey. In blessing, He will bless you, and your child, and the people who are waiting. That is the promise of the Lord.

"When thou goest out . . . be not afraid . . . for the Lord thy God is with thee. . . . Let not your hearts faint, fear not, and do not tremble, neither be ye terrified. . . . For the Lord your God is he that goeth with you" (Deuteronomy 20:1, 3–4).

WHAT *YOU* NEED TO KNOW:

- In blessing He will bless you.
- In multiplying He will multiply you.
- He will hold nothing back from you.
- There will be an angel and a ram in the thicket.

WHAT *YOU* NEED TO DO:

- Climb the mountain, build the altar, and lay out the wood.
- Be willing to sacrifice.
- Hold back nothing from the Lord.
- Trust.

WHAT *YOU* NEED TO BE:

"And she vowed a vow, and said, O Lord of hosts, if thou wilt indeed look on . . . thine handmaid, and remember me, and not forget thine handmaid, but wilt give unto thine handmaid a man child, then I will give him unto the Lord all the days of his life . . . and the Lord remembered her" (1 Samuel 1:11, 19).

CHAPTER 14

HOMEWARD BOUND
Emily Freeman

"And they were firm in the faith of Christ, even unto the end."
ALMA 27:27

The writer Richard Bach once said, "Do not be dismayed at good-byes. A farewell is necessary before meeting again, and meeting again is certain for those who are friends." There is comfort that comes from this certainty; missionaries do come home. We have a great responsibility as mothers in these coming-home moments, a responsibility as great as the preparation that took place before our missionaries left.

Returning from a Full-Time Mission

It is not our privilege to witness the reunion of Ammon and the sons of Mosiah with their parents after their mission to the Lamanites. Oh, what a sweet moment that must have been. But we do receive great insight on what that coming-home conversation must have been like when we read Alma 26. I love how these missionaries describe the process in which they learned to become instruments in the hands of the

Lord. They talk about working with their might, all the day long. They testify of the strength that comes from the Lord through His enabling power—grace. We read about finding comfort in trials, having patience, and enduring suffering. The words in this chapter of scripture allow us to visualize the moments when these missionaries journeyed from house to house: "We have entered into their houses and taught them, and have taught them in their streets; yea, and we have taught them upon their hills" (Alma 26:29). These missionaries were mocked, spit upon, and imprisoned, and they knew what it meant to be delivered. They learned how to have great love. At the end of the chapter, Ammon expresses two sentiments that tell us how important his mission experience had been: "This is my life" and "Now this is my joy, and my great thanksgiving" (Alma 26:36–37).

Take a few minutes and consider what we know about those four boys before their mission experience. Were those four boys the same boys they had been when they left on their mission? No! They had been changed. They had met with kings, served countries, and influenced lives. Their experiences had been extraordinary. Now think about this: what if, when they returned home, their parents treated them as the boys they had been before they left? What if they constrained them to the same rules and boundaries? What if they made their decisions for them rather than letting them be led by the Spirit? It is easy for parents to do, because we are used to the old patterns. Somehow we need to see these returned missionaries as the people they have become and not let them slip back into the people they used to be.

Doing this requires us to step back. Sometimes it requires us to remind our children what they are capable of. When they come to us to solve a problem, rather than telling them what we would do, we must remember to ask, "How would you have handled this on your mission? What process would you have gone through to find your answer?" Most often it will require helping them turn to the scriptures, to prayer, to the Lord. It will require us to allow them to live what they have learned. One of my sons returned home to a closet full of basketball shorts and T-shirts. It had been his favorite attire before he left. On his first morning home he came down and said, "These clothes will not work. My mission president asked me to dress for success, to reflect what I have learned. These clothes don't do that." What amazing insight. Sometimes enabling our missionaries to be who they have become will require supporting change.

The conversations that take place in the days and weeks just following a return are so important. This is your chance to hear about your children's mission experience, but more important, to come to understand the person they have become. Alma 26 is a powerful chapter that recounts the learning that takes place over those years. Our missionaries need to have that same Alma 26 experience. When did they learn to become an instrument in the Lord's hands? What was it like working with their might all day long? What did they learn about grace, about trials, about patience, about comfort? What was it like being in the homes of those they were teaching? This experience has been their life, their joy, and their great thanksgiving for the past eighteen months or two years. Take the time to immerse yourself in the memories of their experience. Just listening to a twenty-minute report in sacrament meeting is not sufficient to understand who they have become. Ask questions, be willing to listen, seek to understand. Most missionaries return and say, "This has been the best two years of my life." Why? Asking probing questions will help us better understand who our missionary children have become.

- What did you love about your companions?
- Which area was the hardest?
- Which area taught you the most?
- What did you learn from your mission president that you never want to forget?
- What did you love about the people you served?
- What was your favorite part of companionship study?
- What did you learn about love, change, or courage?

- How did your relationship with Jesus Christ grow?
- What can you teach me about the Atonement?

In our home we have shared these things in several ways. We schedule a special family home evening for the missionary to share photos and experiences. Another tradition we have is to go on a family trip for a couple days just after the missionary returns home. We plan a small trip, not far from home, where we can listen with no time restraints and no distractions. One other tradition that you might want to consider: on the last week of our children's missions I sent a letter with one request. I asked them to write their own "Alma 26" chapter as their final letter home to our family. Those letters are some of the most precious possessions I have. These opportunities allow us to understand who our child became as a missionary for the Lord. For the rest of their lives, our job is to remind them of who they became on their mission and what they have the potential to be because of that experience.

I received some great advice from a wise mission president. He explained that a missionary has been living a life that required great effort, long hours, hard work, and continual learning. The most important transition we can encourage them in when they return home is to find a job, attend college, and become active in their ward. This allows them to continue right where they left off, with hard work, intense learning, and spiritual growth.

"May the Lord bless you to go forward humbly, prayerfully, and worthily to the mission field and serve as instruments in bringing many souls to him. Know clearly that there are hundreds of thousands who have done so, who have served and are serving faithfully and worthily in the work of the Lord. While you are young, set a pattern of worthiness and faithful service. Do so with all of your heart, and the Lord will greatly bless you, not only in the mission field, but through the rest of your life, your temple marriage, and right into the eternities" (Gene R. Cook, "Worthy to Serve," *New Era,* May 1994, 8).

Our returned missionaries need to hold on to the lesson they learned and the potential they arrived at during their mission. They need to remember the great blessing of their mission as they look forward. Those reminders will bless them as they seek out a companion, prepare for a temple marriage, and continue on their forward path.

If we want our children to continue forth with the same potential they left their mission with, our responsibility is to recognize that level of potential and then encourage them to continue to progress.

WHAT THEY NEED TO KNOW:

- They have become different people from when they left.
- They can receive answers at home the same way they did on their mission.
- It is important to continue to seek out opportunities for hard work, intense learning, and spiritual growth.
- Sharing their experiences will be of great benefit both to themselves and to others.

WHAT THEY NEED TO DO:

- Reflect on their mission.
- Share experiences.
- Express gratitude.
- Write down their memories.
- Continue the daily habit of prayer, scripture study, and service.
- Find a job.
- Attend college.
- Accept callings.
- Seek for a worthy companion.
- Continue to attend the temple.

WHAT THEY NEED TO BE:

"Behold I say unto you, how great reason have we to rejoice; for could we have supposed when we started . . . that God would have granted unto us such great blessings? And now, I ask, what great blessings has he bestowed upon us? Can ye tell? . . . Have we not reason to rejoice? . . . For this is my my life and my light, my joy and my salvation" (Alma 26:1–2, 35–36).

Missionary Letter

"I REMEMBER when I started my mission—I heard about the difficulties I would be facing in an Eastern European country. You can't baptize there, the average missionary baptizes 0.4 people. The country is filled with Catholicism, communism, deep-rooted tradition. Immorality and pornography abound. Hatred and grief still remain from the war. Work hard, be obedient, but don't expect much.

"I never liked hearing that. I came on a mission to help people accept the gospel of Jesus Christ. It wasn't always easy, but I knew the promise was always present, 'Go amongst thy brethren . . . and bear with patience thine afflictions, and I will give unto you success' (Alma 26:27).

"I have been amongst them. I've gone from house to house, building to building. I've spent long hours on the street. It's been freezing cold, with snow blowing horizontally because of the Bura wind. Other times it's been roasting hot, with humidity higher than a boy from Lehi, Utah, had ever imagined. I've been cast out, made fun of, spit upon. I've been yelled at and sworn at. Doors have been slammed, companions have been punched, and rude gestures have been made. But when I think about the last two years, those things don't really come to mind. I think about the lives I've seen change. I think about the times when I've seen a mostly empty church building filled. I remember when something I said struck the heart of a struggling father. I think of the first sincere prayers offered by an overwhelmed doctor, who for the first time recognized that she had a Father in Heaven. I think of families on the path to eternal life, marriages repaired, lives put back into place. The Savior lives. I have never seen the prints in his hands or in his feet, but I have seen him heal. I believe in miracles. I've never seen a man raised from the dead, but I've seen Him work in other ways. He is a God of miracles. I know that this Church is true. I've seen the priesthood exercised by righteous men. No other religion has that. Joseph Smith was a prophet of God. We have a fullness of the truth in this Church, because revelation has not ceased. It continues today, through a living prophet. The Book of Mormon is God's word. I love that book. I love this work. I will never forget this experience. I have been changed. I have accessed and felt the Atonement of Jesus Christ."

CONCLUSION

I won't forget the email I received from my son just months before he returned home from his mission in Croatia. It was 3:35 a.m. in Lehi, Utah, when I heard the email chime. 11:35 a.m. in Zagreb, Croatia. I rolled over and opened the email. Just as I finished reading, the email chimed once again.

The subject read "Ruined Things."

The message was simple: "I don't need new ones, but you can decide . . . it's almost over."

The photos that came with the email brought tears to my eyes. It wasn't the holes in the soles of his shoes that provoked the tears. Nor the stitching coming undone just there above the toe. What became crystal clear in that moment is how many miles my son had walked over the past two years. How many neighborhoods he had passed through. How many doors he had knocked. Day after day after day. Until his shoes were worn through, and used up, and worn out. And if this was how his shoes looked, then how must his heart look? The words of a familiar hymn whispered through my soul: "More used would I be . . ." (*Hymns,* no. 131).

I was reminded of a passage of scripture in Luke: "And he said unto his disciples, Therefore I say unto you, Take no thought for your life, what ye shall eat; neither for the body, what ye shall put on. . . . Consider the lilies how they grow: they toil not, they spin not; . . . If then God so clothe the grass, . . . how much more will he provide for you, if ye are not of little faith? . . . Seek ye the kingdom of God; and all these things shall be added unto you. . . . For where your treasure is, there will your heart be also. Let your loins be girded about, and your lights burning" (JST Luke 12:22–35).

My mind filled with the memories of the moments our hearts had treasured over the past two years, all the things that had been added unto us from this experience. The blessings the Lord had provided. The lilies in the field. What an absolutely tremendous experience it had been. And then I rolled back over in bed and pictured my son, half a world away, who laced up those worn shoes on that morning, girded up his loins, and with his light burning, began to walk.

When my son returned home, I put those shoes in my office as a reminder of the calling I have as a mother—to prepare each of my children for the great work the Lord has in store for them. He has the same calling in store for you. Perhaps this book has given you some courage, wisdom, and insight for the journey ahead. Oh, I hope it has.

We have reached the end of our journey together. More than anything, we hope that your heart has been lifted and that you have felt encouraged. Our prayers will be with you as you continue on this journey of mothering your children and preparing them to serve the Lord. Perhaps you will be led to help others who also find themselves on this journey— allowing this conversation to continue on from mother heart to mother heart. Then we will indeed become a group of women working together to prepare our children for the momentous task ahead.

Hopefully this learning has not been overwhelming to you. Instead perhaps you can look at the things you have learned as stepping stones on your path, lessons that you can consider one by one. As you make this a matter of prayer, we know that you will be inspired and directed by our Heavenly Father as to those things that you can implement now in the lives of your children and those things that should be considered later. We know that you will be guided differently and uniquely for each child.

One thing is certain; the Lord *will* bless you and your children as you continue this preparation process. He will take your offering and will compensate for anything else your children need as they step forward to willingly serve Him. This is His work, a work that is hastening, and His desire for your children to serve is as great as yours.

What a glorious work we have to do. What a divine privilege. Just as it surely was for the Stripling Mothers, the work will be hard and will require us to spend many hours on our knees. But one day we will send our children out into the world to fulfill their missions and their destiny, whatever that may be.

Perhaps our children will have the opportunity to welcome some of our brothers and sisters into the fold of God. What a wonderful blessing that would be. Maybe we will have the opportunity to meet them, either in this life or in the life hereafter. Surely it will be a day of thanksgiving as they, in turn, thank us, the mothers who prepared the missionaries who found them—our children.

Children who did not doubt.

Children who were strengthened by mothers who knew.

"We do not doubt *our mothers knew it.*"

(Alma 56:48; emphasis added)

MEET THE AUTHORS

MERRILEE BOYACK is a high-energy woman who loves life, her family, and her Savior. She is an estate-planning attorney who conducts her law practice from home. Merrilee is also a professional lecturer, featured for many years at BYU Education Week and Time Out for Women. She is the author of several books and talks, including *The Parenting Breakthrough, Strangling Your Husband Is Not an Option, 52 Weeks of Fun Family Service, In Trying Times, Just Keep Trying,* and many more. Her perfect day includes camping and hiking with her family and eating s'mores by a fire. Merrilee and her husband, Steve, live in Lehi, Utah. They have four sons, a daughter-in-law, and two grandchildren. Their sons have served in a variety of ways: Connor served in the Honduras Tegucigalpa Mission, Brennan did humanitarian work in Zambia with Mothers without Borders, Parker served in the Brazil Curitiba Mission, and Tanner served in the Mexico Cuernavaca Mission.

EMILY FREEMAN took her first creative writing class in high school and has loved writing ever since. She finds great joy in studying the life and teachings of Jesus Christ. Her deep love of the scriptures comes from a desire to find their application in everyday life. She is the author of several books, including *21 Days Closer to Christ, Love Life and See Good*

Days, and *Becoming His.* There is nothing Emily enjoys more for breakfast than a bowl of vanilla ice cream, raspberries, and chocolate chips. Other favorites include parades, vacations, firework displays, and going for a long walk with a good friend. Emily and her husband, Greg, live in Lehi, Utah, with their four children, whom she adores. Two of her children have served missions so far: Caleb served in the Adriatic North Mission and Josh served in the Georgia Atlanta Mission. Two sons brought to their family through love have served as well—Garrett served in the Colorado Colorado Springs Mission and Ian is currently serving in the Indiana Indianapolis Mission.

DEANNE FLYNN is the lucky mother of seven amazing kids and two adorable bunnies. She craves ethnic foods, comfy flip flops, and all things C. S. Lewis. She is the author of *The Time-Starved Family: Helping Overloaded Families Focus on What Matters Most, The Mother's Mite: Why Even Our Smallest Efforts Matter,* and *Salt Lake City,* and she speaks frequently to groups nationwide (including BYU's Especially for Youth and Deseret Book's Time Out for Women). After graduating from Brigham Young University in broadcast journalism, DeAnne enjoyed working as a news anchor and reporter. Now, tackling her current job—"The Supreme Manager of Busy Lives" (A.K.A. "Mom")—she and her husband, Craig, and their children (ages 11–24) reside near Salt Lake City. Three of her children so far have served missions: Nick served in the Mexico Monterrey West Mission, Sarah served in the Honduras Tegucigalpa Mission, and Jacob is currently in the Italy Rome Mission.

ROSEMARY RICHARDS LIND grew up in American Fork, Utah, and has a BA degree in English education from BYU. She taught English at Eisenhower Junior High for two years before the birth of her first child, Emily. She has spent the last few years serving on a Church writing committee and travels with her obstetrician husband, Brent, who teaches newborn resuscitation skills with LDS Charities in developing countries. They have thirteen grandchildren with two more on the way. Seven of their eight children have served missions: Scott in the Hungary Budapest

Mission; Jeff in the Ireland Dublin Mission; Marianne in the Spain Madrid Mission; Gary in the Dominican Republic Santiago Mission; Matt in the Switzerland Zurich Mission; Suzy in the Argentina Buenos Aires North Mission; and their youngest, Stephen, is currently serving in the North Carolina Charlotte Mission.

LESLIE OSWALD served with her husband as he presided over the California Ventura Mission. She has six children and twenty-eight grandchildren and lives in Lehi, Utah. Her two sons served missions; McKinley served in Neuquen Argentina and JJ served in Cochabamba Bolivia. Leslie graduated from the University of Utah in Elementary Education. She has been a speaker at BYU Women's Conference. She is currently serving with her husband, who is a district president in the Provo Utah Missionary Training Center.

WENDY ULRICH, PhD, MBA, was a psychologist in private practice in Ann Arbor, Michigan, for almost fifteen years before serving with her husband as he presided over the Canada Montreal Mission. They then moved to Alpine, Utah, where Wendy founded Sixteen Stones Center for Growth, offering seminar-retreats for LDS women. Wendy is a mother and grandmother, a former president of the Association of Mormon Counselors and Psychotherapists, and has been a visiting professor at Brigham Young University. Her books include *Forgiving Ourselves, Weakness Is Not Sin*, national bestseller *The Why of Work* (coauthored with Dave Ulrich), and *The Temple Experience*. Her three children all served missions: Carrie served in the Bulgaria Sofia Mission, Monika in the Taiwan Taichung Mission, and Mike in the Canada Vancouver Mission.

INDEX

INDEX

INDEX